PLAY ON SHAKESPEARE

King John

PLAY ON SHAKESPEARE

All's Well That Ends Well	Virginia Grise
Antony and Cleopatra	Christopher Chen
As You Like It	David Ivers
The Comedy of Errors	Christina Anderson
Coriolanus	Sean San José
Cymbeline	Andrea Thome
Edward III	Octavio Solis
Hamlet	Lisa Peterson
Henry IV	Yvette Nolan
Henry V	Lloyd Suh
Henry VI	Douglas P. Langworthy
Henry VIII	Caridad Svich
Julius Caesar	Shishir Kurup
King John	Brighde Mullins
King Lear	Marcus Gardley
Love's Labour's Lost	Josh Wilder
Macbeth	Migdalia Cruz
Measure for Measure	Aditi Brennan Kapil
The Merchant of Venice	Elise Thoron
The Merry Wives of Windsor	Dipika Guha
A Midsummer Night's Dream	Jeffrey Whitty
Much Ado About Nothing	Ranjit Bolt
Othello	Mfoniso Udofia
Pericles	Ellen McLaughlin
Richard II	Naomi Iizuka
Richard III	Migdalia Cruz
Romeo and Juliet	Hansol Jung
The Taming of the Shrew	Amy Freed
The Tempest	Kenneth Cavander
Timon of Athens	Kenneth Cavander
Titus Andronicus	Amy Freed
Troilus and Cressida	Lillian Groag
Twelfth Night	Alison Carey
The Two Gentlemen of Verona	Amelia Roper
The Two Noble Kinsmen	Tim Slover
The Winter's Tale	Tracy Young

King John

by
William Shakespeare

Modern verse translation by
Brighde Mullins

Dramaturgy by
Katie A. Peterson and Drew Barr

Arizona Center
for Medieval and
Renaissance Studies
ACMRS PRESS
Arizona State University
Tempe, Arizona
2023

———

*Publication of Play On Shakespeare is assisted by
generous support from the Hitz Foundation.
For more information, please visit* www.playonshakespeare.org

———

Published by ACMRS Press
Arizona Center for Medieval and Renaissance Studies,
Arizona State University, Tempe, Arizona
www.acmrspress.com

Library of Congress Cataloging-in-Publication Data
Names: Mullins, Brighde, author. | Peterson, Katie, 1974- contributor. | Barr,
    Drew, contributor. | Shakespeare, William, 1564-1616. King John.
Title: King John / by William Shakespeare ; modern verse translation by
    Brighde Mullins ; dramaturgy by Katie A. Peterson and Drew Barr.
Description: Tempe, Arizona : ACMRS Press, 2024. | Series: Play on
    Shakespeare | Summary: "King John navigates the political twists and turns
    of early English monarchy through this modern translation that parses
    Shakespeare's language carefully, with a focus on its sonic qualities"--
    Provided by publisher.
Identifiers: LCCN 2023030599 (print) | LCCN 2023030600 (ebook) |
    ISBN 9780866987950 (paperback) | ISBN 9780866987967 (ebook)
Subjects: LCSH: John, King of England, 1167-1216--Drama. | Great Britain--
    History--John, 1199-1216--Drama. | LCGFT: Historical drama.
Classification: LCC PR2878.K38 M85 2024 (print) | LCC PR2878.K38
    (ebook) | DDC 812/.6--dc23/eng/20230811
LC record available at https://lccn.loc.gov/2023030599
LC ebook record available at https://lccn.loc.gov/2023030600

Printed in the United States of America

We wish to acknowledge our gratitude
for the extraordinary generosity of the
Hitz Foundation

∽

Special thanks to the Play on Shakespeare staff
Lue Douthit, President and Co-Founder
Taylor Bailey, Producing Director
Cheryl Rizzo, Business Director
Artie Calvert, Finance Director

∽

Originally commissioned by the
Oregon Shakespeare Festival
Bill Rauch, Artistic Director
Cynthia Rider, Executive Director

SERIES PREFACE
PLAY ON SHAKESPEARE

In 2015, the Oregon Shakespeare Festival announced a new commissioning program. It was called "Play on!: 36 playwrights translate Shakespeare." It elicited a flurry of reactions. For some people this went too far: "You can't touch the language!" For others, it didn't go far enough: "Why not new adaptations?" I figured we would be on the right path if we hit the sweet spot in the middle.

Some of the reaction was due not only to the scale of the project, but its suddenness: 36 playwrights, along with 38 dramaturgs, had been commissioned and assigned to translate 39 plays, and they were already hard at work on the assignment. It also came fully funded by the Hitz Foundation with the shocking sticker price of $3.7 million.

I think most of the negative reaction, however, had to do with the use of the word "translate." It's been difficult to define precisely. It turns out that there is no word for the kind of subtle and rigorous examination of language that we are asking for. We don't mean "word for word," which is what most people think of when they hear the word translate. We don't mean "paraphrase," either.

The project didn't begin with 39 commissions. Linguist John McWhorter's musings about translating Shakespeare is what sparked this project. First published in his 1998 book *Word on the Street* and reprinted in 2010 in *American Theatre* magazine, he notes that the "irony today is that the Russians, the French, and other people in foreign countries possess Shakespeare to a much greater extent than we do, for the simple reason that they get to enjoy Shakespeare in the language they speak."

This intrigued Dave Hitz, a long-time patron of the Oregon Shakespeare Festival, and he offered to support a project that looked at Shakespeare's plays through the lens of the English we speak today. How much has the English language changed since Shakespeare? Is it possible that there are conventions in the early modern English of Shakespeare that don't translate to us today, especially in the moment of hearing it spoken out loud as one does in the theater?

How might we "carry forward" the successful communication between actor and audience that took place 400 years ago? "Carry forward," by the way, is what we mean by "translate." It is the fourth definition of *translate* in the Oxford English Dictionary.

As director of literary development and dramaturgy at the Oregon Shakespeare Festival, I was given the daunting task of figuring out how to administer the project. I began with Kenneth Cavander, who translates ancient Greek tragedies into English. I figured that someone who does that kind of work would lend an air of seriousness to the project. I asked him how might he go about translating from the source language of early modern English into the target language of contemporary modern English?

He looked at different kinds of speech: rhetorical and poetical, soliloquies and crowd scenes, and the puns in comedies. What emerged from his tinkering became a template for the translation commission. These weren't rules exactly, but instructions that every writer was given.

First, do no harm. There is plenty of the language that doesn't need translating. And there is some that does. Every playwright had different criteria for assessing what to change.

Second, go line-by-line. No editing, no cutting, no "fixing." I want the whole play translated. We often cut the gnarly bits in

Shakespeare for performance. What might we make of those bits if we understood them in the moment of hearing them? Might we be less compelled to cut?

Third, all other variables stay the same: the time period, the story, the characters, their motivations, and their thoughts. We designed the experiment to examine the language.

Fourth, and most important, the language must follow the same kind of rigor and pressure as the original, which means honoring the meter, rhyme, rhetoric, image, metaphor, character, action, and theme. Shakespeare's astonishingly compressed language must be respected. Trickiest of all: making sure to work within the structure of the iambic pentameter.

We also didn't know which of Shakespeare's plays might benefit from this kind of investigation: the early comedies, the late tragedies, the highly poetic plays. So we asked three translators who translate plays from other languages into English to examine a Shakespeare play from each genre outlined in the *First Folio*: Kenneth took on *Timon of Athens,* a tragedy; Douglas Langworthy worked on the *Henry the Sixth* history plays, and Ranjit Bolt tried his hand at the comedy *Much Ado about Nothing.*

Kenneth's *Timon* received a production at the Alabama Shakespeare in 2014 and it was on the plane ride home that I thought about expanding the project to include 39 plays. And I wanted to do them all at once. The idea was to capture a snapshot of contemporary modern English. I couldn't oversee that many commissions, and when Ken Hitz (Dave's brother and president of the Hitz Foundation) suggested that we add a dramaturg to each play, the plan suddenly unfolded in front of me. The next day, I made a simple, but extensive, proposal to Dave on how to commission and develop 39 translations in three years. He responded immediately with "Yes."

My initial thought was to only commission translators who translate plays. But I realized that "carry forward" has other meanings. There was a playwright in the middle of the conversation 400 years ago. What would it mean to carry *that* forward?

For one thing, it would mean that we wanted to examine the texts through the lens of performance. I am interested in learning how a dramatist makes sense of the play. Basically, we asked the writers to create performable companion pieces.

I wanted to tease out what we mean by contemporary modern English, and so we created a matrix of writers who embodied many different lived experiences: age, ethnicity, gender-identity, experience with translations, geography, English as a second language, knowledge of Shakespeare, etc.

What the playwrights had in common was a deep love of language and a curiosity about the assignment. Not everyone was on board with the idea and I was eager to see how the experiment would be for them. They also pledged to finish the commission within three years.

To celebrate the completion of the translations, we produced a festival in June 2019 in partnership with The Classic Stage Company in New York to hear all 39 of them. Four hundred years ago I think we went to *hear* a play; today we often go to *see* a play. In the staged reading format of the Festival, we heard these plays as if for the first time. The blend of Shakespeare with another writer was seamless and jarring at the same time. Countless actors and audience members told us that the plays were understandable in ways they had never been before.

Now it's time to share the work. We were thrilled when Ayanna Thompson and her colleagues at the Arizona Center for Medieval and Renaissance Studies offered to publish the translations for us.

I ask that you think of these as marking a moment in time.

The editions published in this series are based on the scripts that were used in the Play on! Festival in 2019. For the purpose of the readings, there were cuts allowed and these scripts represent those reading drafts.

The original commission tasked the playwrights and dramaturg to translate the whole play. The requirement of the commission was for two drafts which is enough to put the ball in play. The real fun with these texts is when there are actors, a director, a dramaturg, and the playwright wrestling with them together in a rehearsal room.

The success of a project of this scale depends on the collaboration and contributions of many people. The playwrights and dramaturgs took the assignment seriously and earnestly and were humble and gracious throughout the development of the translations. Sally Cade Holmes and Holmes Productions, our producer since the beginning, provided a steady and calm influence.

We have worked with more than 1,200 artists in the development of these works. We have partnered with more than three dozen theaters and schools. Numerous readings and more than a dozen productions of these translations have been heard and seen in the United States as well as Canada, England, and the Czech Republic.

There is a saying in the theater that 80% of the director's job is taken care of when the production is cast well. Such was my luck when I hired Taylor Bailey, who has overseen every reading and workshop, and was the producer of the Festival in New York. Katie Kennedy has gathered all the essays, and we have been supported by the rest of the Play on Shakespeare team: Kamilah Long, Summer Martin, and Amrita Ramanan.

All of this has come to be because Bill Rauch, then artistic director of the Oregon Shakespeare Festival, said yes when Dave

Hitz pitched the idea to him in 2011. Actually he said, "Hmm, interesting," which I translated to "yes." I am dearly indebted to that 'yes.'

My gratitude to Dave, Ken, and the Hitz Foundation can never be fully expressed. Their generosity, patience, and unwavering belief in what we are doing has given us the confidence to follow the advice of Samuel Beckett: "Ever tried. Ever failed. No matter. Try again. Fail again. Fail better."

Play on!

Dr. Lue Douthit
CEO/Creative Director at Play on Shakespeare
October 2020

WHAT WAS I THINKING?
Brighde Mullins

I was standing on a dirt mound near a field of squash at dusk. I was teaching at Deep Springs, a small liberal arts college and working ranch in a remote valley near the California/Nevada border. I was supposed to be helping pick squash, but instead I was chatting with Dave Hitz, a Silicon Valley mastermind, who was the Chairman of the Board of Trustees at the time. I'd been drinking again. As Dave told me this idea about translating Shakespeare's plays into English, I knew he could tell what I thought. I'm no poker face, even under the best circumstances. I held the aesthetic high ground about *never messing with Shakespeare*. I was skeptical about the whole idea of translating Shakespeare into English. Translate Shakespeare into English? Didn't Shakespeare invent English? The idea, as I understood it, would amuse some and infuriate others. I thought of the title of a John Ashbery poem: *Purists Will Object*.

A year later I was standing in my agent's office in midtown, in NYC, and my agent beamed at me. I was being offered a commission to "*translate a Shakespeare play into English.*" My heart sank. I hate disappointing my agent. As his most unsuccessful client he has stuck by me, and I wanted to be excited. But I couldn't be excited because I had a relationship with Shakespeare's language that precluded the possibility of changing any of it. It all started with Hal's soliloquy:

> *I know you all and will awhile uphold / The unyoked humor of your idleness / but herein will I imitate the sun / Who doth permit the base contagious clouds / to smother up his beauty from the world....*

I first read those lines when I was 20 years old, trapped in a body that didn't work very well, living in a city I loathed. The text of the play was oxygen, it was light, it was mystery. That was the impact of that play on my self-loathing-self in that time and place. It was in *the language* that the meaning resided. Not in any critical interpretation or innovative production, but in the language in and of itself. The meaning was innate in the heft of syllable, of the familiar and the unfamiliar up against each other, and in the mode of thought. Hal's present self was talking to the missing others and through speech was a new self, a self that was free of others. I understood that impulse from the first time I first read those words. I was a 242 lb. woman who lived in Las Vegas, Nevada at a time before body-positivity. I was land-locked, physically, psychologically, and spiritually.

Since the words of Hal in *Henry 4, Part 1* caught my interest, and to some extent, saved me, was it a betrayal of my connection to Shakespeare to mess with the thing that saved me in the first place, i.e., his language? I can be a pretentious person. I'm not proud of that. I had briefly studied with Harold Bloom (may he rest in peace) and I was afraid of what he would think (he was still alive at the time). Because I'm always of several minds about everything I also thought *what's the problem, the play will still exist.* I brought the question of "Translating Shakespeare into English" into my Contemporary Drama class at U.S.C. *Sounds great*, my students said, *sounds amazing. Do this project* they said. I listen to my students. They seem to know what I do not know.

During a conversation with Lue Douthit, the director of the project, who had street credibility as the longtime dramaturg at the Oregon Shakespeare Festival, I remembered a line from T. S. Eliot: "The most we can hope for is to be wrong about Shakespeare in a new way." I had not thought of that quote for years, it was buried in the back of my mind, but something Lue said reminded me, and I took that reminder as a permission slip. I was in.

The next obstacle was which play. My favorite play, *Henry 4, Part 1* was taken. Lue suggested *King John*, a good choice, I secretly thought, because I could do limited damage on a play that was among the least produced if not the least produced of all of Shakespeare's plays. Reading it the first time was a slog — until I met the Bastard and discovered an unlikely connection between *Henry 4* and *King John*: Hal and the Bastard had similar linguistic energies. Hal created a self via language to slip through the pain of misapprehension. What appealed to me about the Bastard was a similar capacity: He revels in new versions of himself and in the capricious fact that a change-of-name gives him more privilege.

The Bastard's second soliloquy is the most famous language in the play: In it he takes others (and himself) to task for the fact that we worship *commodity*, a word we think we know, it doesn't seem as obscure as many of the words in the play. But we don't fully know the word. The word *commodity* is now layered over with meanings and implications Shakespeare did not have in mind — or did he? Shakespeare anticipated Freud. He probably anticipated Marx. The Bastard's language isn't the language of Hal. It's less available and it needs glossing. In his soliloquies, the Bastard moves through waves of self-appraisal. He becomes self-aware and self-conscious. He has been found to be the illegitimate son of Richard the Lionhearted, and is a Plantagenet, therefore he has access to a world of privilege. This access casts him into conundrum after conundrum. This knowledge gives him the chance to step back and imagine himself in new scenarios, to see what he might become. And he vows to fit in, to be part of the world in a new way: He will court commodity, or as we translated it: self-interest. It is hard to understand this basic internal shift because the language, which is the essence of character, is beyond our reach. What is it that still so endlessly satisfies me about language, syllable, sound? Even now it sustains me.

One of the parameters of the project was that I was able to work with a dramaturg. I clicked my heels because I love working with dramaturgs. I asked my old friend Katie Peterson, a Harvard-educated poet with a free attitude toward the text. The play was written in blank verse, one of only five of Shakespeare's plays written in blank verse, and that meant that every line was iambic pentameter. Katie's mantra was that if the translation scanned it was okay. Katie flew to New York (where I was living at the time). Three bottles of wine and two days later we'd "translated" the first few scenes of the play. We cooked up a rewrite with Kardashians and other contemporary folks showing up. Katie and I thought it was hilarious, and while Lue was amused, it wasn't the assignment. The Kardashians had to go.

I needed to start over, but Katie was a trickster poet, and I needed a purist. I did need help. Because every time I tried to work on the play, I fell asleep. Years past I had worked with Drew Barr on a production of *A Midsummer Night's Dream*. Drew was a purist and would be a corrective to our (Katie and mine's) irreverent take. Drew was game, thank God. That summer I was teaching again at Deep Springs, and Drew Barr and I did a cold reading of the original play. The students showed up in Elizabethan ruffs made of coffee filters, with makeshift props filched from the boneyard. I watched Hamza Hussan, a student from Somaliland, read the erstwhile Prince, the one who jumps to his death. Hamza loved the language, and he has since become a poet. Imagination has contaminating powers.

The history plays are about the question of legitimacy and *King John* is part of that thematic pattern. Why and how do certain people get to be in charge and why do others find themselves locked in a tower? There's a wealth of pageantry and a few incredibly intimate scenes that explore this question. My favorite moments are when Constance sinks to the ground, when Arthur pleads for his life, and anytime the Bastard opens his mouth to speak. The play is not understandable unless you have not only an *Oxford English Dictionary*. but also a grasp on many of the facets of that medieval world. It was while I was working on the play with Drew that I fell in love with that world, and not just the Bastard, though the deep dive into the Bastard's commodity soliloquy was the turning point. I was captivated by the wronged Constance and even Cardinal Pandulf whom I loathed at first because he never stops talking. In the end I ended up loving all of them — once I understood their language.

My re-discovery was that which is obvious: So much of the language is obscured by references we no longer understand. *Translation* then maybe wasn't the right word, maybe it was more like a *renovation* or *transliteration* — because there were so many examples of language that needed updating. In these post-Harry Potter times the references to basilisks could stand, but there was much that needed parsing, including all of the language of Cardinal Pandulf whose language sometimes defied logic. There were monologues that were pile-ups of sentences, montages of language in the way that a film will have a montage of images that have immediate associations for a viewer, these word-barrages had meaning for Elizabethans, but for a contemporary reader they were just a word salad that scanned.

Drew sat with several dictionaries; I sat with several editions of the play; and we went over the original word by word till we untangled it as best we could. Our goal: that someone listening to it for the first time — *not reading it, not studying it* — someone *listening* to it might understand it. Might hear it without tuning out. Might stay tuned to the immense pleasure of it, the fortuitous juxtapositions of the fates of these characters.

When I first started writing plays, and seeing them performed, I thought of each production as a form of publication. When a text is published, it is fixed in time, it's been caught, like a bug in a jar.

It stays there inert, no air. After working on *King John*, I realized that this analogy was faulty. No production is definitive. Each production of a play is a form of translation, not a publication. The beautiful difficulty of a play is that *it co-exists with itself*, as written and as performed. When I think about translation, I think about the multiple ways that languages co-exist. The fact that a poem has been translated into another language doesn't obliterate the original poem. This text of *King John*, then, co-exists with the original. I defer on what to call our text of *King John*. A translation, a transliteration, a come-back, a call and response, a linguistic reinvention, an updating, a scanned-update, a side-by-side, a second take on the text. Drew Barr and I did our best, and here it is.

CHARACTERS IN THE PLAY

(*in order of speaking*)

KING JOHN, King of England

CHATILLON, French ambassador to England

QUEEN ELEANOR, the Queen-mother, Henry II's widow

EARL OF ESSEX, English nobleman

BASTARD (PHILIP FAULCONBRIDGE), Richard I of England's natural son (also known as Philip the Bastard and Richard Plantagenet)

ROBERT FAULCONBRIDGE, the Bastard's half-brother; Sir Robert Falconbridge's legitimate son

LADY FAULCONBRIDGE, Philip and Robert's mother; Sir Robert Faulconbridge's widow

JAMES GURNEY, Lady Faulconbridge's attendant

KING PHILIP, King of France

ARTHUR, Lady Constance's son and King John's nephew

DUKE OF AUSTRIA

LADY CONSTANCE, Geoffrey II's widow

BLANCHE OF CASTILE, King John's niece

CITIZEN OF ANGIERS

FRENCH HERALD

ENGLISH HERALD

LEWIS THE DAUPHIN, King Philip's son

EARL OF SALISBURY, English nobleman

CARDINAL PANDULPH, legate from Pope Innocent III

HUBERT, citizen of Angiers and King John's follower

EARL OF PEMBROKE, English nobleman

MESSENGER

PETER POMFRET, a prophet

CHARACTERS IN THE PLAY

LORD **BIGOT**, Earl of Norfolk

VISCOUNT OF **MELUN**

PRINCE HENRY, King John's son, later King Henry III

Other Soldiers, a Sheriff, Citizens, Executioners, Trumpeters,
     Lords, Attendants

ACT 1 ◆ SCENE 1
KING JOHN'S PALACE

Enter King John, Queen Eleanor, Pembroke, Essex, and Salisbury,
with Chatillon, ambassador of France

KING JOHN

Now say, Chatillon, what would France with us?

CHATILLON

I greet you and I speak as King of France
In my behavior to the majesty,
The stolen majesty, of England here —

QUEEN ELEANOR

A strange beginning: "stolen majesty"!   5

KING JOHN

Silence, good mother. Listen to him speak.

CHATILLON

Philip of France, in right and true behalf
Of your late older brother Geoffrey's son,
Arthur Plantagenet, lays most lawful claim
To this fair island and its colonies,   10
To Ireland, Poitiers, Anjou, Touraine, Maine,
And orders you to lay aside your claim,
Which holds unlawfully the deeds to these,
And put the same into young Arthur's hands,
Your nephew and right royal sovereign.   15

KING JOHN

What happens if we disagree with this?

CHATILLON

The proud control of fierce and bloody war,
To enforce these rights so forcibly withheld.

1

KING JOHN
> We'll give you war for war and blood for blood,
> Controlment for control. Tell that to France. 20

CHATILLON
> Then take my king's defiance from my mouth,
> The farthest limit of my embassy.

KING JOHN
> Bring my defiance back and go in peace.
> Be quick as lightning in the eyes of France —
> Before you can report, I will be there; 25
> The thunder of my cannon shall be heard.
> Get out. You'll be the trumpet of our wrath
> And sullen prophet of your own decay.
> Escort him safely to the border, please.
> Pembroke, look to it. Farewell, Chatillon. 30

> *Chatillon and Pembroke leave*

QUEEN ELEANOR *(aside to King John)*
> What now, my son! Have I not always said
> How that ambitious Constance would not stop
> Till she had fired up France and all the world
> Upon the so-called birthright of her son?
> This might've been prevented and resolved 35
> With very easy arguments of love,
> Which now the people of two kingdoms must
> Arbitrate with fearful bloody conflict.

KING JOHN *(aside to Queen Eleanor)*
> Our strong possession and our right for us.

QUEEN ELEANOR *(aside to John)*
> Your strong possession much more than your right, 40
> Or else it will go wrong for you and me —
> So much my conscience whispers in your ear,
> Which none but heaven, and you, and I, shall hear.

ACT 1 ◆ SCENE 1

Enter a Sheriff, who whispers into Essex's ear

ESSEX

My liege, here is the strangest controversy

I have ever heard, come from the country   45

To be judged by you. Shall I bring them in?

KING JOHN

Let them approach.

Exit Sheriff

(to his mother)

Those fat cat priests and monks will bear the cost

Of our just war in France!

Enter Robert and the Bastard

What men are you?   50

BASTARD (PHILIP FAULCONBRIDGE)

Your faithful subject, I'm a gentleman,

Born in Northamptonshire, the oldest son,

So I've been told, to Robert Faulconbridge —

A soldier, by the honor-giving hand

Of Coeur-de-Lion knighted in the field.   55

KING JOHN *(to Robert Faulconbridge)*

And who are you?

ROBERT

The son and heir to that same Faulconbridge.

KING JOHN

You are the older, but you are the heir?

You had not the same mother then, it seems.

BASTARD

Most certain the same mother, mighty King.   60

That is well known — and, as I think, one father;

But, for the certain knowledge of that truth

You need to talk to God — or else my mom.

I have my doubts, as all men's children may.

3

QUEEN ELEANOR

    You watch your tongue, rude man! You shame your mother   65

    And wound her honor with your impudence!

BASTARD

    I, madam? No, I have no impudence.

    It is my brother's claim; it isn't mine.

    If he can prove it, then he cheats me out

    Of at the least five hundred pounds a year.   70

    Heaven guard my mother's honor and my land!

KING JOHN

    A good blunt fellow. Why, being younger born,

    Does he lay claim to your inheritance?

BASTARD

    Once he has slandered me with bastardy,

    He'll get my land with ease. I bet that's why.   75

    Now, whether I'm as true conceived or not,

    That I still lay upon my mother's head;

    But that I am as well conceived, my liege —

    God bless the bones that took the pains for me —

    Compare our faces and then judge yourself.   80

    If old Sir Robert did conceive us both,

    And were our father, and this son like him,

    Oh, old Sir Robert, on my knee, it's true:

    I thank God I look not a thing like you!

KING JOHN

    Why, what a joker heaven sent us here!   85

QUEEN ELEANOR *(to John)*

    He has the look of Coeur-de-Lion's face;

    The accent of his tongue is like him too.

    Do you not read some features of my son

    In the great composition of this man?

KING JOHN *(to Eleanor)*

    My eyes have studied every inch of him   90

    And find him perfect Richard. *(to Robert)* Young man, speak,

    What moves you to come claim your brother's land?

BASTARD

    He is a chinless wonder like his dad.

    With that half-face, he would have all my land;

    His half-face earns five hundred pounds a year!   95

ROBERT

    My gracious liege, when he was still alive,

    Your brother did employ my father much —

BASTARD

    Well, sir, by this you cannot get my land:

    Your tale must be how he employed our mother.

ROBERT

    — And once dispatched him as ambassador   100

    To Germany, there with the emperor

    To treat of high affairs touching that time.

    The King took full advantage of his absence

    And in the meantime stole my father's place;

    Where how he did prevail, I'm shamed to speak.   105

    But, truth is truth: large lengths of seas and shores

    Lay between my father and my mother

    When this same lusty gentleman was got.

    Upon my father's deathbed, he bequeathed

    His lands to me, and took it on his death   110

    That this my mother's son was none of his;

    For, if he were, he came into the world

    Full fourteen weeks before he was expected.

    So let me have what's mine by right, good King:

    My father's land, as was my father's will.   115

KING JOHN

Robert, your brother is legitimate.
Your parents were already legally wed
And, if she did play false, the fault was hers,
Which fault lies on the hazards of all husbands
That marry wives. Tell me, what if my brother,   120
Who as you say took pains to have this son,
Had from your father claimed this son as his?
By law, good friend, your father might have kept
This calf, bred from his cow, from all the world.
The law says, even if he were my brother's,   125
My brother might not claim him; nor, your father,
Though unrelated, refuse him. In brief:
My mother's son did get your father's heir;
Your father's heir will get your father's land.

ROBERT

Then shall my father's will be of no force   130
To dispossess this child which is not his?

BASTARD

Of no more force to dispossess me, sir,
Than was his will to get me, as I think.

QUEEN ELEANOR

What would you rather be: a Faulconbridge
And like your brother to enjoy some land,   135
Or, the reputed son of Coeur-de-Lion,
Lord of your presence, and no land beside?

BASTARD

Madam, let's say my brother had my shape
And I was stuck like him with dad's physique;
Say both my legs were spindly pogo sticks,   140
My arms such eel-skins stuffed, my face so thin
That in my ear I dare not stick a twig

Lest I look like a scarecrow in the field;
If it took that to inherit all his land,
May lightning strike me dead upon this place,   145
I'd give up all that land to have my face.
I'd not be "Pencil Dick" in any case.

QUEEN ELEANOR

I like you well. Will you forsake your fortune,
Give up your land to him and follow me?
I am a soldier and now bound for France.   150

BASTARD

Brother, you take my land. I'll take my chance.
Your face receives five hundred pounds a year;
It's worth more like five farthings, though, I fear.
Madam, I'll follow you unto my death.

QUEEN ELEANOR

Oh no, I'm in no hurry, you go first.   155

BASTARD

But, Madam, I am just a country bumpkin —

KING JOHN

What's your name?

BASTARD

Philip, my King, so is my name begun,
Philip, good old Sir Robert's wife's first son.

KING JOHN

Let's name you after him you look most like —   160
Kneel down as Philip, but rise up more great,
Arise Sir Richard, and Plantagenet.

                    Philip kneels
              King John dubs him a knight,
          tapping him on the shoulder with his sword

BASTARD *(rising, to Robert)*

Brother by our mother, give me your hand:

My father gave me honor, yours gave land.
Now blessèd be the hour, by night or day,   165
When I was got, Sir Robert was away!

QUEEN ELEANOR
The very spirit of Plantagenet!
I am your grandam, Richard; call me so.

BASTARD
Grandma! If it is true or not, who cares?
What's that they say: "a little from the right,   170
Sneak in the window, if you can't lift the latch;
Who dares not woo by day must screw by night,
And have is have, however men do catch."
Near or far off, well shot is well received,
And I am I, no matter how conceived.   175

KING JOHN (to Robert)
Go, Faulconbridge, now you've got your desire;
A landless knight makes you a landed squire.
Come, mother, and come, Richard, we must speed
For France, for France, for it is more than need.

BASTARD
Brother, adieu; good fortune and good luck,   180
For you're the product of an honest fuck.

Exit all but the Bastard

I think that I have grown a full foot taller;
I gained in honor what I lost in land.
Now, I can make any girl a lady.
"Good day, sir Richard!" "How's it hanging, pal?"   185
And if his name be George, I'll call him Hal;
For nouveau riche don't bother learning names;
It's too demeaning and it's too much work
For my new status. Now, wherever I dine,
I'll pick my teeth and loudly slurp my soup;   190

8

And when my knightly stomach is sufficed,
I'll proudly burp while I interrogate
Some foreign dignitary: "My dear sir,"
Thus leaning on my elbow I'll begin,
"I wonder what you've heard them say of me?"   195
— That is the question now, since I'm in charge!
And then his answer all pro forma goes:
"You know, my dear sir, I'm at your command,
At your employment, at your service, sir";
"No, sir," I counter, "I, sweet sir, at yours";   200
And so, we'll talk in circles through the night
And cut each other off being polite,
Bragging about the mountains we have seen,
Our foreign travels on some swanky cruise,
We'll draw toward sunrise in conclusion so.   205
But look, man, this is how the other half lives
And fits the mounting spirit like myself.
For, he is but a bastard to the time
That does not smack of such civility
And, so I am, whether I smack or not;   210
And, not just in my clothing and my bling,
Exterior form, outward accoutrement,
But, from an inward motion, I'll deliver
Sweet, sweet, sweet poison for the age's tooth.
For, though I will not practice to deceive,   215
Yet, to avoid deceit, I mean to learn;
And that shall pave the way for my new self.
          Enter Lady Faulconbridge and James Gurney
But who comes in such haste in riding clothes?
What woman post is this? Has she no husband
That will prepare her entrance and her way?   220
Dear God, it is my mother. How now, mom?

9

What brings you out in public dressed like that?
LADY FAULCONBRIDGE
　Where is that wretch your brother? Where is he
　Maligns my honor up and down the street!
BASTARD
　My brother Robert? He who looks like dad?   225
　Nimrod the Giant, your husband Robert's son?
　Is it Sir Robert's son you're looking for?
LADY FAULCONBRIDGE
　"Sir Robert's son?" Yes, you irreverent boy,
　Sir Robert's son! Why do you scorn Sir Robert?
　He is Sir Robert's son, and so are you!   230
BASTARD
　James Gurney, could you give us leave awhile?
GURNEY
　Good leave, good Phillip.
BASTARD
　Phillip? Who is he?
　You're so behind the times, old family friend.
　I'll fill you in once I have talked with mom.   235

Exit Gurney

　Mother, I am not old Sir Robert's son;
　Sir Robert might have ate his part of me
　And still not broken his Good Friday fast.
　Sir Robert would be lucky — face the facts —
　To get to say that he resembled me;   240
　We've seen his handiwork. Therefore, good mother,
　To whom am I beholden for these limbs?
　You obviously slept with someone else.
LADY FAULCONBRIDGE
　Have you conspired with your brother too?
　You should defend my honor for your sake.   245

10

Why do you scorn me, you ungrateful knave?

BASTARD

"Knight, knight," good mother, shining-armor-like.
Look! I am "dubbed" — I have it on my shoulder.
See, mother, I am not Sir Robert's son;
I have disclaimed Sir Robert and my land;   250
Legitimation, name, and all are gone.
Mother, please, tell me who my father was —
Some proper man, I hope. Who was it, mom?

LADY FAULCONBRIDGE

Have you denied yourself a Faulconbridge?

BASTARD

As faithfully as I deny the devil.   255

LADY FAULCONBRIDGE

King Richard Coeur-de-Lion was your father.
By long and vehement suit, I was seduced
To make room for him in my husband's bed.
Heaven don't blame my child for my trespass!
You are the issue of my dear offense,   260
Which was so strongly forced past my defense.

BASTARD

Now, by this light, were I begot again,
Madam, I would not wish a better father. ·
Some sins bear out their privileges on Earth,
Though not in Heaven. Your fault was not your folly.   265
You had to place your heart at the dispose
Of him against whose fury and brute force
The awesome lion could not win the fight.
Whoever dares to say you did not well
When I was got, I'll send his soul to hell.   270
Come, lady, I will show you to my kin;
And they shall say, when Richard me begot,

11

If you had just said no, it had been sin.
Who says it was, he lies. For, it was not.

They exit

ACT 2 ♦ SCENE 1
FRANCE. BEFORE ANGIERS
Flourish

Enter before Angiers, a town in France, King Philip of France,
Lewis the Dauphin, Constance, Arthur, and their forces on one side;
Duke of Austria, wearing a lion's skin, and his forces on the other

KING PHILIP

Before Angiers well met, brave Austria.
Arthur, that great forerunner of your blood —
Richard, who robbed the lion of his heart —
By this brave duke came early to his grave.
And, in apology to Richard's kin,   5
At our importance Austria has come
To pledge allegiance, child, on your behalf
And to prevent the hostile takeover
By your unnatural uncle, English John.
Embrace him, love him, give him welcome here.   10

ARTHUR *(to Austria)*

God will forgive you Coeur-de-Lion's death
Because you choose to give his children life,
Sheltering their right under your wings of war.
I give you welcome with a powerless hand,
But with a heart full of unstainèd love.   15
Welcome before the gates of Angiers, Duke.

KING PHILLIP

A noble boy. Who would not treat you well?

AUSTRIA *(to Arthur)*

I lay this zealous kiss upon your cheek
A seal to prove the contract of my love:

That to my home no more will I return 20
Till Angiers and the right you have in France
Is safe from any foreign influence,
Even till England, utmost corner of the West,
Salutes you for her king. Till then, fair boy,
I will not think of home, I'll think of war. 25

CONSTANCE

Oh, take his mother's thanks, a widow's thanks,
Till your strong hand shall help to give him strength
To make a more requital to your love.

AUSTRIA

The peace of heaven is theirs that lift their swords
In such a just and charitable war. 30

KING PHILIP

Let's get to work. Our cannon shall be aimed
Against the brows of this resisting town.
We'll lay our royal bones before Angiers,
With Frenchmen's blood we'll flood the marketplace,
But we will make it subject to this boy. 35

CONSTANCE

Wait for an answer from your messenger,
Lest ignorant you stain your swords with blood.
My lord Chatillon may bring from England
That right in peace which here we urge in war,
And then we should repent each drop of blood 40
That hot rash haste so indirectly shed.

Enter Chatillon

KING PHILIP

A wonder, lady! Look, upon your wish,
Our messenger, Chatillon, is arrived.
What England says say briefly, gentle lord;
We calmly wait for you; Chatillon, speak. 45

CHATILLON

    England, impatient with your just demands,

    Has armed himself. The adverse winds

    Whose leisure I have stayed, have given him time

    To land his legions all as soon as I.

    He's right around the corner from this town,   50

    His forces strong, his soldiers confident.

    With him the Mother Queen is brought along,

    Like Ate, ancient goddess of all strife;

    With her her niece, the Lady Blanche of Spain;

    With them a bastard of the Lion King   55

    And all the angry jobless of the land —

    Rash, inconsiderate, fiery young recruits

    Who gambled everything to come to war,

    Bearing their birthrights proudly on their backs

    To take a risk and find their fortunes here.   60

(drum beats)

    The interruption of their churlish drums

    Cuts short my repartee. See, here they come.

KING PHILIP

    How much unlooked for is this expedition.

AUSTRIA

    Unlooked for, unexpected — by as much

    We must awake endeavor for defense,   65

    For courage rises with occasion.

    Let them be welcome, then. We are prepared.

        Enter King John, Bastard, Queen Eleanor, Blanche,

        the Earl of Pembroke, Salisbury, and the English forces

KING JOHN

    Peace be to France, if France, in peace, permit

    Our possession of what belongs to us.

    If not, we will bleed France and peace will fly;   70

While we, God's wrathful agent, castigate
The lot of those who beat his peace to heaven.
KING PHILIP
  Peace be to England, if you take war back
  From France to England and stay there in peace.
  England we love, and, for that England's sake,   75
  With burden of our armor here we sweat.
  This job we're doing should be done by you,
  But you're so far away from loving England
  That you have undermined its lawful king,
  Cut off the sequence of the family line,   80
  Intimidated and committed rape
  Upon the maiden virtue of the crown.
  Look here upon your brother Geoffrey's face.
(he points to Arthur)
  These eyes, these brows, were molded out of his;
  This little abstract replicates that large   85
  Which died with Geoffrey, and the hand of time
  Will draw this brief into as huge a volume.
  That Geoffrey was your older brother born,
  And this his son; England was Geoffrey's right
  And this is Geoffrey's. In the name of God   90
  How comes it then that you are called a king,
  When living blood does in these temples beat
  Which own the crown that you have dared to steal?
KING JOHN
  Who gives you jurisdiction in this case
  To make me answer your unfounded claims?   95
KING PHILIP
  God, the heavenly judge that stirs good thoughts
  In any breast of strong authority
  To look into the blots and stains of right.

That judge has made me guardian to this boy,
And under his warrant I impeach your wrong,   100
And with his help I mean to punish you.

KING JOHN
Beware; you do usurp authority.

KING PHILIP
I must do so to beat usurping down.

QUEEN ELEANOR
Who is it that you call usurper, France?

CONSTANCE
Let me make answer. *(to Eleanor)* Your usurping son.   105

QUEEN ELEANOR
Out, insolent! Your bastard shall be king
That you may be a queen and check the world.

CONSTANCE
My bed was ever to your son as true
As yours was to your husband; and this boy
Liker in feature to his father, Geoffrey,   110
Than you to John, whose manners are like yours —
Like rain to water, devil to his dam.
My boy, a bastard? By my soul, I think
His father wasn't as so true conceived;
He simply couldn't be, since you're his mom.   115

QUEEN ELEANOR
There's a good mother, boy, that blots your father.

CONSTANCE
There's a good grandma, boy, that would blot you.

AUSTRIA
Peace!

BASTARD
Hear the crier!

AUSTRIA

Who the hell are you?   120

BASTARD

One that will play the devil, sir, with you,

Who'll snatch that lion's skin when you're alone.

You're like the bunny, as the saying goes,

Who bravely plucks dead lions by the beard.

I'll burn your skin-coat, if I catch you right.   125

Watch out! I'm coming for you! Here I come!

BLANCHE

Who wore it best? Richard the Lionhearted,

Who first disrobed that lion. Not this fool.

BASTARD

It looks as stupid on the back of him

As Hercules's shoes upon an ass.   130

But, ass, I'll take that burden from your back,

And lay on that shall make your shoulders crack.

AUSTRIA

What cracker is this same who deafs our ears

With such abundance of superfluous breath?

Quickly, King Philip, tell us what to do.   135

KING PHILIP

Women and fools, break off your conference.

King John, perhaps I'll spell it out for you:

England and Ireland, Anjou, Touraine, Maine,

In right of Arthur I do claim from you.

Will you forfeit them and lay down your arms?   140

KING JOHN

My life as soon! I do defy you, France.

Arthur of Brittany, yield up to my hand,

And out of my dear love I'll give you more

Than e'er the coward hand of France can win.

Submit then, boy.   145

QUEEN ELEANOR *(to Arthur)*

Come to your grandma, child.

CONSTANCE

Yes, child, surrender to your grandmother.

Give grandma your whole kingdom. Grandma will

Give you a plum, a cherry, and a fig.

There's a good grandma.   150

ARTHUR

Good my mother, peace.

I wish that I were laid low in my grave.

I am not worth this trouble made for me.

QUEEN ELEANOR

His mother shames him so, poor boy, he weeps!

CONSTANCE

Shame upon you whether I do or not!   155

His grandma's wrongs and not his mother's shames

Draw tears from his eyes like heaven-moving pearls,

Which heaven shall take as if they were a fee.

Yes, with these crystal beads heaven is bribed

To do him justice and revenge on you.   160

QUEEN ELEANOR

You monstrous slanderer of heaven and earth!

CONSTANCE

You monstrous "injurer" of heaven and earth,

Don't call me "slanderer" when you usurp

The territories, royalties, and rights

Of this oppressed boy, your oldest grandson,   165

Unfortunate in nothing but in you.

Your sins are visited on this poor child.

He will live out the letter of God's law,

Being but the second generation

Sep'rated from your sin-conceiving womb.   170

KING JOHN

Crazy! Stop this.

CONSTANCE

I've just got this to say:

That he's not only damnèd for her sin,

But, God has made her sin, and her, the plague

On this unlucky offspring: plagued for her   175

And by her plagued; her sin his injury,

Her injury the payment for her sin,

All punished in the person of this child,

And all because of her. A plague on her!

QUEEN ELEANOR

You ignorant bitch, I can at once produce   180

A will that voids the title of your son.

CONSTANCE

Oh, who doubts that? A will? A wicked will,

A woman's will, a crooked grandma's will!

KING PHILLIP

Peace, lady; pause, or be more temperate;

It does not suit us to play umpire for   185

You harpies screeching repetitions.

Hey, trumpet player, summon to the walls

These men of Angiers. Let us hear them speak

Whose title they admit, Arthur's or John's.

Trumpet sounds

Enter a Citizen of Angiers upon the walls

CITIZEN

Who is it that has called us to our walls?   190

KING PHILIP

It's France, for England.

20

KING JOHN

England, for itself.

You men of Angiers and my loving subjects —

KING PHILIP

You loving men of Angiers, Arthur's subjects,

Our trumpet called — let's have a little talk —   195

KING JOHN

For our advantage. Therefore, hear us first.

These flags of France that are advancèd here

Before the eye and prospect of your town

Have made this march for your endangerment.

Their cannons have their bowels full of wrath   200

And they are ready mounted to spit forth

Their iron indignation against your walls.

But on the sight of us, your lawful king,

The French, amazèd, want a "little talk";

And now, instead of bullets wrapped in fire,   205

They shoot words, like blanks, that go up in smoke

To blow a faithless promise in your ears,

Which, you must disbelieve, kind citizens,

And let us in. I am your king. My spirits

Exhausted in this action of swift speed,   210

Requests safe harbor in your city's walls.

KING PHILIP

When I have said, make answer to us both.

(Philip takes Arthur by the hand)

Look! In this right hand, whose protection

Is most divinely vowed upon the right

Of him it holds, stands young Plantagenet,   215

Son to the older brother of this man

And king over him and all that he enjoys.

For Arthur's stolen and downtrodden rights,

21

We march in armed battalion against your town;
We are no further enemy to you.   220
So, pay that duty which you truly owe
To him that owns it, namely, this young prince;
And then our guns are like a muzzled bear,
They might look scary but they don't cause harm.
Our cannons' malice vainly shall be spent,   225
Against th' invulnerable clouds of heaven
And with a blessèd and un-vexed retreat,
With un-hacked swords and helmets all unbruised,
We will bear home that lusty blood again
Which we were set to spill upon your town   230
And leave your children, wives, and you, in peace.
But listen up: if you refuse this deal,
Not even the circumference of your walls
Will save you from our messengers of war.
Then, tell us, shall your city call us lord?   235
That's what we ask, desire, and demand.
This is the turning point: should we fire first
And spill your blood to get what's really ours?
CITIZEN
    In brief: we are the King of England's subjects.
    For him, and in his right, we hold this town.   240
KING JOHN
    Acknowledge me your king, and let me in.
CITIZEN
    That we cannot. But he that proves the king,
    To him we will prove loyal. Till that time
    Have we rammed up our gates against the world.
KING JOHN
    Does not the crown of England prove the king?   245
    And if not that, I bring you witnesses:

Twice fifteen thousand hearts of England's breed —

BASTARD *(aside)*

Bastards included!

KING JOHN

To verify my title with their lives.

KING PHILIP

We have an equal number for the French —   250

BASTARD *(aside)*

Some bastards, too, no doubt.

KING PHILIP

Stand in his face to contradict his claim.

CITIZEN

Till you can prove whose right is worthiest,

We will withhold our town from either side.

KING JOHN

Then God forgive the sins of all those souls   255

That to their everlasting residence,

Before the dew of evening fall, will rush

In dreadful trial of our kingdom's king.

KING PHILIP

Amen, amen. Get on your horses, knights!

BASTARD

Saint George that thrashed the dragon, and ever since   260

Sits on his horseback on my tavern's door,

Teach us to fight! *(to Austria)* Mister, if I were now

At your place, mister, with your lioness,

I'd put the cuckold's horns upon your head

And make a monster of you.   265

AUSTRIA

Peace! No more.

BASTARD

Oh tremble, for you hear the lion roar.

KING JOHN

On top of yonder hill, we'll set up camp

And organize our eager regiments.

BASTARD

Speed, then, to take advantage of the field.   270

KING PHILIP

It shall be so; and at the other hill

Command the rest to stand. God and our right!

They exit

The Citizen remains

Here, after excursions, enter the French Herald

with Trumpeters, to the gates

FRENCH HERALD

You men of Angiers, open wide your gates,

And let young Arthur, Duke of Brittany, in,

Who, by the hand of France, this day has made   275

Much work for tears in many an English mother,

Whose bleeding sons lie scattered on the ground;

Many a widow's husband lies face-down

Coldly embracing the discolored earth;

And victory at little cost does play   280

Upon the dancing banners of the French,

Who are at hand, triumphantly displayed,

To enter conquerors, and to proclaim

Arthur of Brittany England's king and yours.

Enter English Herald with trumpet

ENGLISH HERALD

Rejoice, you men of Angiers, ring your bells!   285

King John, your king and England's, now approaches,

Commander of this hot malicious day.

His armors, that marched here so silver bright,

Are coming back crusted with Frenchmen's blood.

There stuck no plume in any English crest 290
That is removèd by a sword of France;
Our colors do return in our own hands,
That did display them first when we first marched,
And like a jolly troop of huntsmen come
Our hearty English, with their blood-stained hands, 295
Dyed in the dying slaughter of their foes.
Open your gates and let the winners in.

CITIZEN

Heralds, from our towers we saw every move
From first to last, the scrimmage and retreat
Of both your armies, and who is winning 300
By our keen eyes cannot be determined.
Blood has brought blood, and blows have answered blows,
Strength matched with strength, and power confronted power.
Both are alike, and both alike we like.
One must prove greatest. While you weigh so even, 305
We hold our town for neither, yet for both.

Enter on one side King John, Queen Eleanor, Blanche,
the Bastard, the Earl of Salisbury and English forces;
on the other side, King Philip, Lewis the Dauphin,
Austria, and French forces

KING JOHN

France, have you e'en more blood to cast away?
Say, should the current of our right roam on,
Whose passage, vexed with your impediment,
Will leave its native channel, flood its banks, 310
Overflowing even your walled borders,
Unless you let his silver water keep
A peaceful progress to the ocean?

KING PHILIP

England, you have not saved one drop of blood

In this hot trial more than we of France,   315
Rather lost more. And I swear by this hand
That sways the earth this climate overlooks,
Before we will lay down our just-borne arms
We'll put you down, against our enemies,
Or add a royal number to the dead,   320
Telling the noble story of this war's loss
With slaughter coupled to the name of kings.

BASTARD

Ha, majesty! How high your glory towers
When the rich blood of kings is set on fire!
Now Death smiles at us with a grill of steel;   325
The swords of soldiers are his teeth, his fangs,
And now he feasts, mousing the flesh of men,
In undetermined differences of kings.
Why are your armies just standing around?
Cry "havoc," Kings! Back to the bloody field,   330
You equal potents, fiery kindled spirits.
Then let confusion of one part confirm
The other's peace. Till then, blows, blood, and death!

KING JOHN

Citizens! Whose side will you let in?

KING PHILIP

Speak, citizens, for England. Who's your king?   335

CITIZEN

The King of England, when we know the king.

KING PHILIP

Know him in us that here hold up his right.

KING JOHN

In us that are our own great deputy;
We bear possession of our person here,
Lord of our presence, Angiers, and of you.   340

CITIZEN

    A greater power than we denies you both.

    Until there is no doubt, we will keep locked

    All our concerns in our strong-barrèd gates.

    Kinged by our fears, until our fears are soothed,

    Purged and dethroned by the definitive King.   345

BASTARD

    By Heaven, these punks of Angiers mock you, Kings,

    And stand securely on their balconies

    As in a theater, where they gape and point

    And watch you play out scenes and acts of death.

    Royal presences, do what I say: 350

    Be friends awhile and both conjointly bend

    Your sharpest deeds of malice on this town.

    I'd fire incessantly upon these jades

    Until I'd strip them of their defenses

    And leave them naked in the vulgar air.   355

    That done, dissever your united strengths

    And part your mingled colors once again;

    Turn face-to-face, and bloody sword to sword.

    Then, in a moment, Fortune then shall choose

    Her happy minion from between your sides   360

    To whom in favor she shall give the day,

    And kiss him with a glorious victory.

    How like you this wild counsel, mighty kings?

    Smacks it not something of the policy?

KING JOHN

    Now by the sky that hangs above our heads,   365

    I like it well. France, shall we knit our powers

    And lay this Angiers even with the ground,

    Then after that, we'll fight for who is king?

BASTARD

And if you have the mettle of a king,

Insulted as we are by this rude town,   370

Turn the barrels of your artillery,

As we will ours, against these saucy walls.

And when we've shocked and awed them to the ground,

Then we'll defy each other, and pell-mell

Make work upon ourselves, for heaven or hell.   375

KING PHILIP

Let it be so. Say, where will you assault?

KING JOHN

We from the west will send destruction

Into this city's bosom.

AUSTRIA

I from the north.

KING PHILIP

Our thunder from the south   380

Shall rain their drift of bullets on this town.

BASTARD *(aside)*

A brilliant strategy! From north to south,

Austria and France shoot in each other's mouth.

I'll stir them to it. Come away, away!

CITIZEN

Hear us, great Kings! Let's walk this back a bit,   385

And I shall show you peace and fair-faced league.

You'll win the city without stroke or wound,

Allow your men to die in their own beds

That would've been just cannon fodder here.

Persever not, but hear me, mighty Kings!   390

KING JOHN

Keep going. We are listening to you.

CITIZEN

    That daughter there of Spain, the Lady Blanche,

    Is niece to England. Can you imagine

    The Prince of France with that most lovely maid?

    If lusty love should go in quest of beauty,   395

    Where should he find it fairer than in Blanche?

    If pure love should go in search of virtue,

    Where should he find it purer than in Blanche?

    If ambitious love went looking for a match,

    Whose veins flow richer blood than Lady Blanche?   400

    Such as she is, in beauty, virtue, birth,

    Is the young Dauphin every way complete.

    He is but one half of a perfect soul,

    Left to be finished by someone like her,

    And she a pretty perfect half of him,   405

    Whose fullness of perfection he completes.

    These two such silver currents, when they join,

    Glorify the banks that bound them in;

    Two such controlling shores shall you be, Kings,

    To these two princes, if you marry them.   410

    This marriage will do more than any war

    To open up our walls: for this strong match

    Will dynamite our gates, blow them so wide

    We must give entrance. But without this match,

    The stormy sea itself is not so deaf,   415

    Lions more confident, mountains and rocks

    More free from motion, no, not Death himself

    In mortal fury half so determined,

    As we to keep our city.

        King Philip and Lewis the Dauphin walk aside and talk

BASTARD *(aside)*

    Here's a twist   420

That shakes the rotten carcass of old Death
Out of his rags! Here's a blow-hard indeed
That spits forth death and mountains, rocks and seas,
Talks as familiarly of roaring lions
As maids of thirteen do of puppy dogs.   425
What warrior's behind this lusty talk?
He speaks plain cannon fire and smoke and bang!   '
He tases them; he tortures with his tongue.
Our ears are battered; not a word of his
But buffets better than the fist of France.   430
Christ! I was never so bethumped with words
Since I first called my brother's father dad.

QUEEN ELEANOR *(aside to King John)*
Son, pay attention, listen, make this match.
Give with our niece a dowry large enough,
And by this knot you'll tie and guarantee   435
Your now wobbly assurance to the crown.
I see a yielding in the looks of France.
See how they whisper. Urge them while their souls
Are capable of doing what we say,
Before zeal, melted by the windy breath   440
Of soft petitions, pity, sympathy,
Cool and congeal again to what it was.

CITIZEN
Why don't you answer, double majesties,
This friendly treaty of our threatened town?

KING PHILIP
Speak England first, since you spoke first last time   445
We spoke unto this city. What say you?

KING JOHN
If the Dauphin there, your princely son,
Can in this book of beauty read "I love,"

30

Her dowry will weigh equal with a queen.
We'll gild her bridal bed, and make her rich   450
In titles, honors, and in privilege.

KING PHILIP

Son, what do you say? Look in the lady's face.

DAUPHIN

I do, my Lord, and in her eye I find
A wonder or a wondrous miracle,
I see the shadow of myself in there   455
Which, being but the shadow of your son,
Becomes a sun, and makes me just a shade.
What can I say? I never loved myself
Until just now I see myself through her,
Drawn in the sweet reflection of her eye.   460

He whispers with Blanche

BASTARD *(aside)*

Drawn in the sweet reflection of her eye!
Hanged in the frowning wrinkle of her brow!
And quartered in her heart! He shows that he
Will prove to be love's traitor. What a shame,
That hanged and drawn and quartered, there should be,   465
In such a love, so vile a jerk as he.

BLANCHE *(aside to Dauphin)*

My uncle's will in this respect is mine.
If he sees anything that he approves,
Anything at all in you that's to his liking,
I will with ease translate it to my will.   470
I'll never falsely flatter you, Lewis,
That all I see in you is lovable;
I'll say instead: there's nothing that I see,
Though unkind thoughts themselves would be your judge,
Which I can tell would give me cause to hate.   475

KING JOHN

What say these young ones? Blanche, did you decide?

BLANCHE

It's up to you. I must by honor do

What you in your wisdom would have of me.

KING JOHN

Speak up, Prince Dauphin. Can you love my niece?

DAUPHIN

No, ask me if I can refrain from love,   480

For I do love her most unguardedly.

KING JOHN

Then I'll make you a gift of provinces:

Volquessen, Touraine, Maine, Poitiers, Anjou

Are yours. And I'll throw in some hard cash too,

Thirty thousand pounds, English currency.   485

Philip of France, if this satisfies you,

Then order them to join hands and be wed.

KING PHILIP

It pleases me. Young royals, close your hands.

AUSTRIA

And your lips too, for I am well assured

That I did so when I was first assured!   490

Dauphin and Blanche join hands and kiss

KING PHILIP

Now, people of Angiers, open your gates.

Let the alliance that you made play out,

And at Saint Mary's Chapel presently

The rites of marriage shall be celebrated.

Isn't the Lady Constance in our group?   495

I'm certain she is not, for her presence

Would have thwarted the sealing of this match.

Where's she and little Arthur? Anyone?

DAUPHIN

She's sad and passionate in your highness's tent.

KING PHILIP

And by my faith, this match that we have made   500

Will give her sadness very little cure.

Brother of England, how may we appease

This grieving widow? On her behalf we came,

Which we, God knows, have turned the other way,

To our advantage.   505

KING JOHN

We will heal up all,

Once we pronounce young Arthur Duke of Brittany

And Earl of Richmond, we'll make him lord of

This fair town. Call the Lady Constance.

Some speedy messenger should bring her now   510

To our celebration. *(Salisbury exits.)* I trust we shall,

If not fill up the measure of her will,

Yet in some measure satisfy her so

That we shall stop her exclamation.

Go we as well as haste will suffer us,   515

To this unlooked for, unpreparèd pomp.

All but the Bastard exit

BASTARD

Mad world! Mad kings! Mad goddamn compromise!

John, to stop Arthur's title in the whole,

Has willingly departed with some land

And France, whose armor conscience buckled on,   520

Whom zeal and charity brought to the field

As God's soldier, was flattered and seduced

By that same purpose-changer, that sly devil,

That pimp who slaps honor upside the head,

That daily break-vow, he that wins of all,   525

Of kings, of beggars, old men, young men, maids, —
Who having no external thing to lose
But the word "maid" cheats the poor maid of that —
That smooth-faced, gentleman, commodity,
A.K.A. self interest, sways the world,   530
The world that of itself is balanced well,
Made to run even upon even ground,
Till opportunity presents itself
And mad self-interest, this commodity,
Makes it abandon all indifference,   535
From all direction, purpose, course, intent;
And this same bias, this commodity,
This whore, this pimp, this malleable word,
Clapped on the wandering eye of fickle France,
Seduced him from his spiritual desires,   540
From a resolved and honorable war
To a convenient and pragmatic truce.
And why do I bad-mouth commodity?
Only because he's not seduced me yet.
Not that I'd be able to turn him down   545
If he sent forth an angel with a bribe,
But since my hand goes unattempted yet,
I rant against the rich like a poor beggar.
And while I am a beggar, I will rant
And say there is no sin but to be rich;   550
Though once I'm rich, my virtue then shall be
To say there is no vice but beggary.
Commodity, since kings break faith for you,
Self-interest, you're the boss, I'll worship too.

He exits

34

ACT 3 ◆ SCENE 1

THE FRENCH KING'S PAVILION

Enter Constance, Arthur, and the Earl of Salisbury

CONSTANCE *(to Salisbury)*

Gone to be married! Gone to swear a peace!
Will Lewis get Blanche, and Blanche those provinces?
It isn't so. Say you are mistaken.
It cannot be, you do but say it's so.
I trust I cannot trust you, for your word   5
Is but the vain breath of a common man.
I have a king's oath to the contrary.
You'll be punished for scaring me like this.
For I am sick, susceptible to fears,
Oppressed with wrongs and therefore full of fears.   10
Now, if you were to say this was a prank,
With my vexed spirits I could not settle down,
But I will quake and tremble all this day.
What do you mean by shaking of your head?
Why do you look so sadly on my son?   15
Why do your eyes hold those pathetic tears,
Like proud rivers peering over their banks?
Are these sad signs a kind of guarantee?
Then speak again, not all of your long tale,
But this one word, whether or not it's true.   20

SALISBURY

As true as I believe you think them false
That give you cause to prove my saying true.

CONSTANCE

Oh, if you teach me to believe this sorrow,

35

Then teach this sorrow how to make me die,
And let belief and life encounter so   25
As does the fury of two desperate men,
Who in their very meeting fall and die.
Lewis marry Blanche! My boy, then where are you?
France friends with England, what becomes of me?
Get out! I cannot stand the sight of you.   30
This news has made you a most ugly man.

SALISBURY

What other harm have I done, good lady,
But spoke the harm that is by others done?

CONSTANCE

Which harm within itself is so heinous
As it makes harmful all that speak of it.   35

ARTHUR

I beg of you, please mother, be content.

CONSTANCE

If you who wishes me content were foul,
Speckled with warts and little ugly dots,
Full of unpleasing blots and sightless stains,
Lame, foolish, crooked, sick, prodigious,   40
Covered with moles and eye-offending spots,
I would not care, I would then be content,
For then I should not love you. You would not
Become your great birth, or deserve a crown.
But you're gorgeous, and at your birth, dear boy,   45
Nature and Fortune joined to make you great.
You may, like lilies, boast of Nature's gifts
And like the blooming rose. But fickle Fortune
Has been corrupted, changed, and cheated you,
She's fornicating with your uncle John,   50
And with her golden hand has prodded France

To trample down respect of sovereignty
And made Philip's majesty bawd to them.
France is bawd to Fortune and King John,
That strumpet Fortune, that usurping John!   55
Tell me, good man, is not France a liar?
Defame him with your words, or go away
And leave me with the sadness I alone
Am destined to endure.

SALISBURY

I'm sorry, ma'am,   60

I may not go without you to the Kings.

CONSTANCE

You may, you shall. I will not go with you.
I will instruct my sorrows to be proud,
For grief is proud and makes his owner droop.

(she sinks to the ground)

To the supremacy of my prized grief   65
Let kings assemble, for my grief's so great
That no supporter but the huge firm earth
Can hold it up. Here I and sorrow sit.
This dirt's my throne; let kings come worship it.

Exit Salisbury with Arthur
Constance remains seated on the ground
Flourish
Enter King John, King Philip, Lewis the Dauphin, Blanche,
Queen Eleanor, the Bastard, Austria

KING PHILIP *(to Blanche)*

It's true, fair daughter, and this blessed day,   70
Shall always be a holiday in France.

CONSTANCE

A wicked day, and not a holy day!
What does this day deserve? What has it done

37

That it should be in golden letters set
Among the high tides in the calendar? 75
No, rather, turn this day out of the week,
This day of shame, oppression, perjury.
Or, if it must stay put, let pregnant women
Pray that their babies not be born today,
Because their hopes will be completely lost. 80
And, on this day let sailors know they'll wreck;
All treaties made on this day will be broke;
This day all things begun come to ill end;
And faith itself becomes a desperate lie!

KING PHILIP

By heaven, lady, you will have no cause 85
To curse the fair proceedings of this day.
Have I not pledged my loyalty to you?

CONSTANCE

You have lied to me with a counterfeit
Resembling loyalty, which, tried-and-tested,
Proves to be worthless. You are perjured. Perjured. 90
You came in arms to spill my enemy's blood,
But now in arms you marry it to yours.
The grappling vigor and rough frown of war
Is cold in amity and painted peace,
And my oppression has made up this league. 95
Arm, arm, you heavens, against these perjured kings!
A widow cries; be my husband, God!
Don't let the hours of this ungodly day
Wear out the day in peace; before night falls,
Set armed discord between these lying kings. 100
Hear me! Please, hear me!

AUSTRIA

Lady Constance, peace!

CONSTANCE

    War! War! No peace. Peace is a war to me.

    Oh Limoges of Austria, how you shame

    That lion's skin. You slave, you wretch, you coward,   105

    You're big and strong when on the stronger side;

    You're Fortune's champion, but you only fight

    When her capricious ladyship's nearby

    To grant you safety. You're a liar too,

    Suck-up to greatness. What a fool you are,   110

    A blustering fool, to brag and stamp and swear

    As if on my behalf. You cold-blooded slave,

    Haven't you roared like thunder on my side?

    Been sworn my soldier, bidding me depend

    Upon your stars, your fortune, and your strength?   115

    And now you go over to my enemies?

    You wear a lion's skin! Strip it off, for shame,

    And hang a calfskin on those recreant limbs.

AUSTRIA

    Oh that a man should speak those words to me!

BASTARD

    "And hang a calfskin on those recreant limbs."   120

AUSTRIA

    You dare not say so, villain, or you die!

BASTARD

    And hang a calf's skin on those recreant limbs.

Enter Pandulph

KING PHILIP

    Here comes the pope's holy ambassador.

PANDULPH

    Hail, thou anointed deputies of God!

    To thee, King John, my holy errand is.   125

    I, Pandulph, of fair Milan cardinal,

And from Pope Innocent the legate here,
Do in his name religiously demand
Why thou against the church, our holy mother,
So willfully dost spurn, and force perforce   130
Keep Stephen Langton, chosen Archbishop
Of Canterbury, from his Holy Seat?

KING JOHN

Who do you think you are, you nobody,
To tax the free breath of a sacred king?
You cannot, cardinal, cook up a name   135
So slight, unworthy, and ridiculous
To demand I answer to, as the *pope*.
Tell him this tale, and from the mouth of England
Add this much more, that no eye-talian priest
Shall tax or troll in our dominions;   140
But as we under God are supreme head,
So, under God that great supremacy,
Where we do reign, we will alone uphold
Without the interference of a mere mortal.
So tell the pope, all reverence set apart   145
To him and his bogus authority.

KING PHILIP

Brother of England, you blaspheme in this.

KING JOHN

Though you and all the kings of Christendom
Are stupidly led by this meddling priest,
Dreading a curse that money may erase —   150
For by the merit of vile gold, trash, dust,
You purchase absolution for your sins —
All by myself I fight and I oppose
This papal fake, and count his friends my foes.

40

PANDULPH

    Then, by the lawful power that I have,   155

    Thou shalt stand cursed and excommunicate,

    And blessèd shall be he that doth revolt

    From his allegiance to this heretic;

    And meritorious shall that hand be called,

    Canonized and worshiped as a saint,   160

    That takes away by any secret course

    Thy hateful life.

CONSTANCE

    O, lawful let it be

    That I have room with Rome to curse awhile!

    Good father cardinal, cry out amen   165

    To my loud curses, for without my wrong

    No tongue has any power to curse him right.

PANDULPH

    There's law and warrant, lady, for my curse.

CONSTANCE

    And for mine, too. When law can do no right,

    Let it be lawful I can do no wrong.   170

    Law cannot give my child his kingdom here,

    Since he who holds the kingdom holds the law.

    Therefore, since law itself is perfect wrong,

    How can the law forbid my tongue to curse?

          Philip takes John's hand and holds it forcefully

PANDULPH

    Philip of France, on peril of a curse,   175

    Let go the hand of that arch-heretic,

    And raise the power of France upon his head,

    Unless he do submit himself to Rome.

QUEEN ELEANOR

    You look frightened, France. Don't unclasp your hand.

CONSTANCE *(to Eleanor)*

That's the way, devil, don't let France repent! 180

For by disjoining hands, hell loses a soul.

AUSTRIA

King Philip, listen to the cardinal.

BASTARD

And hang a calfskin on his recreant limbs.

AUSTRIA

Well, ruffian, I must pocket up these wrongs,

Because — 185

BASTARD

You're wearing brand new calfskin pants.

KING JOHN

Philip, what say you to the cardinal?

CONSTANCE

What should he say, but "Amen, cardinal!"

DAUPHIN

Choose wisely father, for the difference

May purchase you a heavy curse from Rome, 190

Versus the loss of England as your friend.

Let go the easier.

BLANCHE

The curse of Rome.

CONSTANCE

Lewis, hold fast, the devil tempts you here,

In likeness of your newly blushing bride. 195

BLANCHE

The Lady Constance speaks not from her faith,

But from her need.

CONSTANCE

Oh, if you grant my need,

Which only lives but by the death of faith,

That need must then imply this principle, 200
My faith may live again by death of need.
Oh then, beat down my need and faith will rise,
Keep my need up and faith stays beaten down.

KING JOHN

You've angered him, he will not answer you.

CONSTANCE *(to King Philip)*

Oh, be removed from John and answer true! 205

AUSTRIA

Do so, King Philip. Hang no more in doubt.

BASTARD

Hang nothing but a calfskin, most sweet kraut.

KING PHILIP

I am perplexed and don't know what to say.

PANDULPH

What canst thou say but will perplex thee more,
If thou stand excommunicate and cursed? 210

KING PHILIP

Good reverend father, make my person yours,
And tell me what you'd do if you were me.
John's royal hand and mine are newly knit
With all religious strength of sacred vows.
When we last spoke, we promised each other 215
Our deep sworn faith, peace, amity, true love
Between our kingdoms and our royal selves,
And even before this truce, minutes before,
Not even long enough to wash our hands
To close this royal bargain up in peace, 220
God knows our hands were bloody and were stained
By slaughter's paint-brush, where revenge did paint
The fearful difference of enragèd kings.
And shall these hands, so lately washed of blood,

43

So newly joined in love, so strong in both,   225
Undo this handshake and this liaison?
Play fast and loose with faith? So joke with heaven,
Make such un-constant children of ourselves,
As now again to snatch our palm from palm,
Unswear faith sworn, and on the marriage-bed   230
Of smiling peace to march a bloody host,
And make a riot on the gentle brow
Of true sincerity? Oh holy sir,
Out of your grace devise, ordain, impose
Some gentle order, then we shall be blessed   235
To do your pleasure and continue friends.

PANDULPH

All form is formless, order orderless,
Save what is opposite to England's love.
Therefore to arms! Be champion of our church.
Or let the church, our mother, breathe her curse,   240
A mother's curse, on her rebellious son,
France, thou mayst seize a serpent by the tongue,
A wounded lion by its tender paw,
A hungry tiger safer by its fangs,
Than keep in peace that hand which thou doth hold.   245

KING PHILIP

I may let go John's hand, but not my oath!

PANDULPH *(to King Philip)*

By holding on, thou forfeit thine true oath
And instigate an inner civil war,
Thy tongue against thy tongue. Oh, let thy vow
First made to God, first be to God performed.   250
That is, be thou the champion of our church.
Thy latest oath was sworn against thyself
And must not be performed against thyself.

For, when what thou hast sworn to do is wrong,
It is not wrong to do what makes it right, 255
And being not done, where doing tends to ill,
The truth is then most done not doing it.
Religion makes thou keep thy holy vows,
But thou hast sworn against religion
And mak'st thine oath a guarantee of truth 260
Against thine faith, swearing to be forsworn.
There is no better conquest thou canst make
Than arm thy constant and thy nobler parts
Against these giddy loose temptations,
Upon which better part our prayers come in, 265
If you accept them. But if not, then know
The peril of our curses light on thee
So heavy as thou shalt not shake them off.

AUSTRIA

Rebellion! Flat, rebel —

BASTARD

Would you shut up? 270
Will not a calfskin stop your big fat mouth?

DAUPHIN

Father, to arms!

BLANCHE

Upon my wedding day?
What, shall our feast be kept with slaughtered men?
Should braying trumpets and loud thumping drums, 275
Clamors of Hell, be measures to our pomp?

(she kneels)

Oh, husband, hear me! Yes, alas, how new
Is "husband" in my mouth! Even for that name,
Which until now my tongue never pronounced.
Upon my knee, I beg, don't go to war 280

45

Against my uncle!

CONSTANCE *(kneeling)*

Oh, upon my knee,

Made hard with kneeling, I do pray to thee,

You virtuous dauphin, alter not the doom

Ordained by heaven!   285

BLANCHE

Now I shall see your love. What motive may

Be stronger with you than the name of wife?

CONSTANCE

That which upholds him and that he upholds

His honor. Oh, your honor, Lewis, your honor!

DAUPHIN

I wonder, father, why you are so cold   290

When such considerations call to you.

PANDULPH

I will pronounce a curse upon your head.

KING PHILIP

There is no need. England, I fall from thee.

Philip lets go of John's hand

CONSTANCE *(rising)*

Oh fair return of banished majesty!

QUEEN ELEANOR

Oh foul revolt of French inconstancy!   295

KING JOHN

France, you'll regret this hour within this hour.

BLANCHE

Which side do I choose, with whom do I go?

I am with both. Each army has a hand,

And in their rage, I'm holding onto both.

They whirl asunder and dismember me.   300

Husband, I cannot pray that you will win.

Uncle, I needs must pray that you will lose.
Father, I may not wish you good fortune.
Grandma, I will not wish your dreams come true.
Whoever wins, on that side I will lose.   305

DAUPHIN

Lady, with me, with me your fortune lies.

BLANCHE

And where my fortune lives, there my life dies.

She goes to him

KING JOHN *(to the Bastard)*

Cousin, it's time to gather up our troops.

Exit the Bastard

France, I am burning with a fiery wrath,
A rage with heat of such extremity   310
That nothing can allay, nothing but blood,
The blood, and dearest-valued blood, of France.

KING PHILLIP

Your rage shall burn you up, and you shall turn
To ashes ere our blood shall quench that fire.
Look to yourself, you are in jeopardy.   315

KING JOHN

No more than he that threatens. Let's go fight!

They exit

ACT 3 ◆ SCENE 2

THE PLAINS NEAR ANGIERS

Alarms. Excursions. Enter the Bastard, with Austria's head.

BASTARD

Now, by my life, this day grows wondrous hot.
Some airy devil hovers in the sky
And pours down mischief. Austria's head stay put
While I catch my breath. *(He throws down head.)*

47

Enter King John, Arthur, and Hubert

KING JOHN

Hubert, watch this boy. Cousin, wake up.   5

My mother was assaulted in her tent

And kidnapped, I'm afraid.

BASTARD

I rescued her.

Her highness is in safety, have no fear.

Let's go, my liege, for very little pains   10

Will bring this labor to a happy end.

Exit (with the others)

ACT 3 ◆ SCENE 3
THE SAME

Alarms, excursions and retreats. Enter King John, Queen Eleanor,
Arthur, the Bastard, Hubert, Lords.

KING JOHN *(to Eleanor)*

So it shall be; your grace shall stay behind

And strongly guarded. *(to Arthur)* Nephew, don't be sad.

Your grandma loves you, and I soon will be

As dear to you as your own father should.

ARTHUR

Oh this will make my mother die of grief!   5

KING JOHN *(to the Bastard)*

Cousin, let's get to England. You go first

Before me, making sure you shake the bags

Of money-grubbing priests and liberate

Their stolen currency. Fat ribs of peace

Will now be eaten clean by my soldiers.   10

Use my authority and all my force.

BASTARD

Bell, book, and candle shall not hold me back

When gold and silver call my name so loud.
I leave your highness. Grandma, I will pray,
If ever I remember to be holy,   15
For your fair safety. So I kiss your hand.

QUEEN ELEANOR

Farewell, gentle cousin.

KING JOHN

Good coz, farewell.

Exit the Bastard

QUEEN ELEANOR

Come here, my little grandson. Come to me.

She takes Arthur aside

KING JOHN

Come here, Hubert. Oh my gentle Hubert,   20
I owe you much. Within this wall of flesh
There is a soul counts you her creditor,
And will repay your love with interest.
My friend, your freely given loyalty
Lives in this bosom, dearly cherishèd.   25
Give me your hand. I had a thing to say,
But I will fit it to a better time.
By heaven, Hubert, I'm almost ashamed
To say how much respect I have for you.

HUBERT

I am indebted to your majesty.   30

KING JOHN

Good friend, you have no cause to say so yet.
But you may have. Right now the time seems wrong,
Yet time will come when you'll get your reward.
I had a thing to say — but let that go.
The sun is shining, and the day is bright,   35
Too full of colors and gaudy displays

For you to pay me mind. When midnight comes,
If we were standing in a graveyard then,
And you were tortured by a thousand wrongs —
If you could see me, really see me,   40
Hear me, really hear me, and you could reply
With just your eyes, using your mind alone,
Without the harmful sounds of words gone wrong —
I could begin to tell you everything.
But I cannot. I love you, you know that.   45
And I suspect you also love me back.

HUBERT

So much so that what you would have me do,
Though that my death followed upon my act,
By heaven, I would do it.

KING JOHN

I know you would.   50
Good Hubert, Hubert, Hubert, turn your eye
To that young boy. I'll tell you what, my friend,
He is a serpent, always in my way,
And wherever I may decide to walk,
He slinks beneath me. Do you understand?   55
You are his keeper.

HUBERT

And I'll keep him so
That he shall not offend your Majesty.

KING JOHN

Death.

HUBERT

My lord?   60

KING JOHN

A grave.

HUBERT

He shall not live.

KING JOHN

Enough.

I could be merry. Hubert, I love you.

But I won't say what I intend for you.   65

Remember.

(turning to Eleanor)

Madam, fare you well.

I'll leave those forces to protect your grace.

QUEEN ELEANOR

My blessing goes with you.

KING JOHN

To England, child.   70

Hubert shall be your man and care for you

With all true duty. On toward Calais, go!

Exit all

ACT 3 ◆ SCENE 4

THE FRENCH KING'S TENT. FRANCE.

Enter King Philip of France, Lewis the Dauphin,
Pandulph, Attendants

KING PHILIP

So, by a roaring tempest out at sea,

Our whole armada of committed ships

Is scattered and completely lost to us!

PANDULPH

Courage and comfort. All shall yet go well.

KING PHILIP

What can go well when we have run so ill?   5

Are we not beaten? Is not Angiers lost?

Arthur's a prisoner? Several allies dead?

And bloody John is back to England gone,
In spite of our resistance on each front?
DAUPHIN
What John has won, he's also fortified.   10
Such swiftness with such prudent judgment met,
Such detached calm in such a fierce contest
Is unprecedented. Who's read or heard
Of anything that's similar to this?
KING PHILIP
I could stand England's fortune and your praise   15
If I could find a shame that equals ours —
(At this exact moment Constance enters. Speak of the devil.
Her hair is a mess. Like she's blown a fuse.)
Look who comes here! A grave unto a soul.
I beg you, lady, come away with me!
CONSTANCE
See, now, the gruesome product of your peace.
KING PHILIP
Patience, good lady. Calm down, Constance, please.   20
CONSTANCE
No, I defy all counsel, all redress,
But that which ends all counsel, true redress.
Death. Death, oh amiable, lovely Death.
The putrid stench, the rancid rot of flesh,
Rise from your coffin's everlasting grave.   25
You are the enemy of happiness,
And I will kiss your detestable bones,
And place my eyeballs in your dull sockets,
And ring my fingers with your corpse's worms,
And stop this mouth of mine with filthy dirt,   30
And be a carrion monster, like yourself.
Come, grin at me, I'll take it that you flirt,

Then French kiss me real slowly. Misery,
Oh, come to me!

KING PHILIP

Oh fair affliction, peace!   35

CONSTANCE

No, I have none, having breath to cry.
I wish my tongue were in the thunder's mouth!
Then with my passion I would shake the world,
And rouse from sleep that dull anatomy
Which cannot hear a lady's feeble voice,   40
And disregards her ordinary cries.

PANDULPH

Lady, you utter madness and not grief.

CONSTANCE

You're far too holy to understand me.
I am not mad. This hair I tear is mine.
My name is Constance. I was Geoffrey's wife,   45
Young Arthur is my son, and he is lost.
I am not mad. I wish to God I were,
For then I simply could forget myself.
Oh, if I could, what grief would I forget!
Preach some theology to make me mad,   50
And you'd be named a saint, dear cardinal,
For being capable of such wild grief,
My reason finds it reasonably reasonable
That I might be relieved of this sadness
And urges me to kill, to hang myself.   55
If I were mad, I'd just forget my son,
Or madly think he was a doll, a toy.
I am not mad. Too well, too well I feel
The different curse of each calamity.

(to King Philip)

    To England, if you will.   60

KING PHILIP

    Bind up your hairs.

CONSTANCE

    Yes, I could do that, but what good is it?

    I tore them from their bonds and cried aloud,

    "Oh, that these hands could so redeem my son,

    As they have given these hairs their liberty."   65

    But now I envy them their liberty,

    And will again commit them to their bonds,

    Because my little boy's a prisoner.

                        She binds up her hair

PANDULPH

    Your overstated grief becomes a sin.

CONSTANCE

    He talks to me who never had a son.   70

KING PHILIP

    You are as fond of grief as of your child.

CONSTANCE

    Grief fills the room up with my absent child,

    Lies in his bed, walks up and down with me,

    Puts on his pretty looks, repeats his words,

    Remembers me of all his gracious parts,   75

    And plumps his empty garments with his form.

    Is that reason enough to love my grief?

    You tell me, if you had a similar loss

    I could give better comfort than you do.

(she unbinds her hair)

    I will not keep this form upon my head   80

    When all my wits are so disorderèd.

    Oh, Lord! My boy, my Arthur, my sweet son,

My life, my joy, my food, my all the world,
My widow-comfort, and my sorrows' cure!

Constance exits

KING PHILIP

I fear she'll harm herself, I'll follow her.   85

He follows her

DAUPHIN

There's nothing in this world that gives me joy.
And bitter shame has spoiled the sweet world's taste.
It yields nothing but shame and bitterness.

PANDULPH

What have you lost by losing of this day?

DAUPHIN

All days of glory, joy, and happiness.   90

PANDULPH

If you had won it, certainly you had.
Listen, when Fortune's really on your side,
She looks at you with her most threatening eyes.
It's strange to think how much King John has lost
In this which he imagines he has won.   95
Are you upset that Arthur's his prisoner?

DAUPHIN

As heartily as he is glad he has him.

PANDULPH

Your naive mind's as youthful as your blood.
Now hear me speak with a prophetic spirit,
John has seized Arthur, and it cannot be   100
That while warm blood's flowing through Arthur's veins
Usurping John will have one minute's peace.
A scepter snatched with an unruly hand
Must be as violently maintained as gained,
And he that stands on such a slippery slope   105

Will go to any lengths to stay upright.
For John to stand, then Arthur needs to fall.
So be it, for it cannot be but so.

DAUPHIN

But what would I gain by young Arthur's fall?

PANDULPH

You, on behalf of Lady Blanche your wife,   110
May now make all the claims that Arthur did.

DAUPHIN

And lose them, life and all, as Arthur did.

PANDULPH

You are naive, and green in this old world.
John's plots against you work on your behalf,
For he who spills true blood for his own safety   115
Shall find but bloody safety, and untrue.
John's act so evilly done shall cool the hearts
Of all his people, freezing up their zeal,
And, given any chance that they can get
To end his reign, they'll surely cherish it.   120

DAUPHIN

Maybe he will not touch young Arthur's life,
But hold him safely in his prison cell.

PANDULPH

Oh, sir, when he will hear of your approach,
If that young Arthur's not already dead,
Even at that news, he dies, and then the hearts   125
Of all John's people shall revolt from him
And kiss the lips of their much longed-for change,
And pick strong matter of revolt and wrath
Out of the bloody fingerprints of John.
In England now offending decency   130
The bastard Faulconbridge ransacks the church.

If but a dozen French were there in arms,
They could incite the English to their side
Just as a little snow, tumbled about,
Someday becomes a mountain. Noble Dauphin, 135
Go with me to your father. Celebrate
What may be made from England's discontent
Now that their souls are doomed by John's offense.
For England, go. I will whip up your king.

DAUPHIN

Strong reasons make strange actions. Let us go, 140
If you say yes, our king will not say no.

They exit

ACT 4 ◆ SCENE 1

A ROOM IN A CASTLE

Enter Hubert and Executioners,
with irons, rope, and other torture devices

HUBERT

Heat up these irons hot, and then go hide
Behind the tapestry. I'll signal you
By tapping my foot twice. Then you rush out
And tie the boy that you will find with me
Tight to that chair. Be careful. Hurry, go!   5

FIRST EXECUTIONER *(as he exits)*

I hope your orders justify your deeds.

HUBERT

My orders are quite clear. Now do my will.

Enter Arthur

Young boy, come here. I need a word with you.

ARTHUR

Good morning, Hubert.

HUBERT

Morning, little Prince.   10

ARTHUR

I'm a little Prince with a big title.
I'll be a "Big" Prince, someday. Are you sad?

HUBERT

Indeed, I have had better days.

ARTHUR

Hubert,
I think nobody should be sad but me.   15
But I remember, when I was in France

59

French teenagers would act like they were sad
To get attention and sympathy — Sheesh!
If I were out of prison and kept sheep
I'd be as happy as the day is long.   20
I'd e'en be happy here except I think
My uncle has a plan to cause me harm.
He is afraid of me, and I of him.
Is it my fault that I was Geoffrey's son?
It isn't, and instead I wish to God   25
I were your son, so you would love me, Hubert.
HUBERT *(aside)*
If I listen to his sweet innocence,
He will awake my mercy which lies dead.
Therefore I will be sudden and act fast.
ARTHUR
Are you sick, Hubert? You look pale today.   30
In truth, I wish you were a little sick,
Then I'd stay up all night and watch o'er you.
I bet I love you more than you love me!
HUBERT *(aside)*
His words take such possession of my heart.
(he shows Arthur a paper)
Read this, young Arthur.   35
(aside)
Here come foolish tears,
Driving all thoughts of torture from my mind.
I must be brief or else I'll lose my nerve
And cry my eyes out like some little girl.
(to Arthur)
Can't you read it? Isn't it fairly writ?   40
ARTHUR
Too fairly, Hubert, for so foul effect.

Must you with hot irons burn out both my eyes?
HUBERT
Young boy, I must.
ARTHUR
And will you?
HUBERT
Yes I will.   45
ARTHUR
You have the heart? When you had a headache,
I wrapped my handkerchief about your brow,
My very best, a princess made for me,
And I never even asked it back from you,
And all night long I cradled your poor head   50
And like the watchful minutes to the hour,
With my good cheer I helped the time to pass,
Asking "What do you need? Where do you hurt?"
Or "What on God's earth can I do for you?"
Many a poor man's son would not have cared   55
And ne'er have spoken one kind word to you,
But you, at your bedside, you had a Prince.
You might think my love was calculated
And crafty, you may think that if you will.
If heaven be pleased that you must use me ill,   60
Why then you must. Will you burn out my eyes?
These eyes that never did or never will
So much as frown at you?
HUBERT
I've sworn to do it.
And with hot irons I must burn them out.   65
ARTHUR
The iron-poker may be made red-hot,
But as it approaches it'll drink my tears

And quench its fiery indignation
Even in the matter of my innocence,
And, after that, will oxidize in rust   70
Because it carried fire into my eyes.
Are you more stubborn-hard than hammered-iron?
'Cause if an angel should have come to me
And told me Hubert should put out my eyes,
I would not have believed him. There's no tongue   75
But Hubert's —

HUBERT *(stamps his signal to the executioners)*

It's time!

> *Enter Executioners with a length of rope, a poker*

Do as I tell you.

ARTHUR

Save me, Hubert, save me! My eyes are out
Even with the scary looks of these hard men —   80

HUBERT

Hand me the poker, now, and tie him up.

> *Hubert takes the iron*

ARTHUR

All right, but do you need to be so rough?
I will not struggle, look, I stand stone-still.
For heaven's sake, Hubert, please make this stop!
No, hear me, Hubert! Send these men away,   85
And I will sit as quiet as a lamb.
I will not move, or wince, or speak one word.
Send these fierce men away and I'll forgive
Whatever suffering you would do to me.

HUBERT *(to executioners)*

Go, stand within. Leave me alone with him.   90

FIRST EXECUTIONER

I am relieved to be away from here.

Exit Executioners

ARTHUR

It looks like I have sent away a friend.

He had a harsh look but a gentle heart.

Let him come back, that his compassion may

Give life to yours.   95

HUBERT

Come boy. Prepare yourself.

ARTHUR

There is no other way?

HUBERT

You'll lose your eyes.

ARTHUR

If only there were a speck in your eye,

A grain, a dust, a gnat, a wandering hair,   100

Then, feeling how small things can cause such pain,

Your vile intent would seem too horrible.

HUBERT

Is this your promise? Stop it, hold your tongue.

ARTHUR

Two tongues together could not even describe

How much is needed this one pair of eyes.   105

Oh, Hubert, if you will, cut out my tongue

So I may keep my eyes. Please, spare my eyes,

Although they have no use but seeing you.

(Arthur seizes the iron)

But, feel this now, the poker is ice-cold

And could not burn me.   110

HUBERT

I can heat it, boy.

ARTHUR

No, you cannot. The fire has died from grief,

Being created for comfort, to be used
In violent extremes. Look for yourself.
There is no malice in this burning coal.   115
The breath of heaven has blown the fire out
And scattered repentant ashes on its head.

HUBERT

But with my breath I can revive it, boy.

ARTHUR

And if you do, you will but make it blush
And glow through shame of your proceedings, Hubert.   120
Or worse. It might send sparks into your eyes,
All things that you should use to do me wrong
Deny their office. Only you do lack
That mercy, which fierce fire and iron extend,
Creatures of note for mercy-lacking uses.   125

HUBERT

Well, see to live. I will not touch your eyes
For all the treasure that your uncle owns.
Yet, I was sworn and charged to do so, boy,
And with this very iron to burn them out.

ARTHUR

Oh, now you look like Hubert! All this while   130
You were disguisèd.

HUBERT

Peace. No more. Be still.
Your uncle must believe that you are dead.
I'll fill these evil spies with false reports.
And, pretty child, sleep free of doubt and sure   135
That Hubert, for the wealth of all the world,
Will never do you harm.

ARTHUR

Thank you, Hubert —

HUBERT

Silence! No more! Go secretly with me.

Much danger do I undergo for thee. 140

Exit all

ACT 4 ◆ SCENE 2

KING JOHN'S PALACE

Enter King John, Pembroke, Salisbury, and other Lords

KING JOHN

Here once again we sit, once again crowned

And looked upon, I hope, with cheerful eyes!

PEMBROKE

This "once again," but that your highness pleased,

Was once superfluous — since crowned before

And your royal title was not removed. 5

SALISBURY

Therefore, to be possessed with double pomp,

To gild refinèd gold, to paint the lily,

To throw more perfume on the violet,

Is wasteful and ridiculous excess.

PEMBROKE

Because your royal whims must be indulged, 10

We have to suffer through this episode,

A coronation we've already seen,

And we don't have the time to watch repeats.

SALISBURY

In this most ancient and most well-known place,

This ceremonial act now looks deformed. 15

It frightens everyone and makes them worry —

KING JOHN

My reasons for my double coronation

I have already told you, they were good.

And more I will reveal when I'm less scared,
Then you will understand. Meantime, just say   20
What you would have me change that is not well
And well shall you perceive how willingly
I will both hear, and grant you your requests.

PEMBROKE

Then I, as one that am the tongue of these,
Do sound the purposes of all our hearts.   25
We recommend the swift release of Arthur.
If what you rule in peace by right you hold,
Why should your fears, which as they say, attend
A guilty conscience, move you to lock up
Your tender kinsman and to choke his days   30
With barbarous ignorance, denying him
The rich advantage of good exercise?
That the crown's enemies may not have cause
To spark rebellion, let it be our suit
As you have bid us ask, his liberty.   35
It is not for our good that we do ask —
Except our good is suited to your own —
It is the best for all to set him free.

KING JOHN

I hear you well. I will release the youth
To your custody.   40

Enter Hubert

Hubert, what's the news?

Hubert whispers to King John

PEMBROKE

This is the man should do the bloody deed.
He showed his warrant to a friend of mine.
The imprint of a wicked heinous act
Still twists his face. If you look close enough,   45

You'll see the traces of a guilty conscience,
And I do fear that we are now too late.
He has already killed him it would seem.

SALISBURY

The color in the King's face comes and goes.
His guilt is like a boil that's 'bout to burst —   50

PEMBROKE

And when it bursts, I fear the pus will be
The foul corruption of that sweet child's death.

KING JOHN (coming forward)

We cannot hold mortality's strong hand.
Good lords, although my will to give is living,
The suit that you demand is gone and dead.   55
He tells me Arthur is deceased tonight.

SALISBURY

Indeed, we feared his sickness was past cure.

PEMBROKE

Indeed, we heard how near to death he was,
Before the child himself felt he was sick.
This must be answered here or in heaven.   60

KING JOHN

Why are you both looking at me like that?
You think I hold the scissors of the Fates?
Do I have power over the pulse of life?

SALISBURY

There seems to be foul play, and it's a shame
That greatness should so grossly order death.   65
So thrive it in your game, and so farewell.

PEMBROKE

Wait up, Lord Salisbury. I'll go with you
And find the resting place of this poor child.
His blood which owned the breadth of this great isle,

Now only owns three feet. Bad world the while! 70
This cannot be contained, it will break out
To all our sorrow, and quite soon, no doubt.

Lords exit

KING JOHN

They burn in indignation. I repent.
There is no sure foundation set on blood,
No certain life achieved by others' death. 75

Enter Messenger

You look terrified. Where is that color
That I have seen inhabit in those cheeks?
So foul a sky clears not without a storm,
Pour down your weather. How goes all in France?

MESSENGER

From France to England, never was such power 80
Of any foreign army on our land
Imposed so fully and so readily.

KING JOHN

What? Are our spies all drinking on the job?
Or are they sleeping? Where's my mother been,
That such an army could have formed in France 85
Without her having heard?

MESSENGER

My lord, her ear
Is stopped with dust. On April first, your noble
Mother died. And I also hear, my lord,
The Lady Constance died by suicide. 90

KING JOHN

Slow down your speed, dreadful occasion!
Oh, spare me more bad news till I have pleased
My discontented peers. What? Mother's dead?
How wildly ruined are my affairs in France!

Under whose command are those French troops   95
You say you've seen, you say are landed here?
MESSENGER
Under the Dauphin.
KING JOHN
You make me dizzy
With all this bad news —
        The Bastard enters with Peter of Pomfret, a prophet
Now, what says the world   100
To your proceedings? Do not seek to stuff
My head with more bad news, for it is full.
BASTARD
But if you are afraid to hear the worst,
Then let the worst, unheard, fall on your head.
KING JOHN
Bear with me, cousin, I was overwhelmed   105
Under the tide, but I've come up for air
Above the flood and can give audience
To any tongue, no matter what it says.
BASTARD
How I have sped among the clergymen
You'll see by how much money I have raised.   110
But also, as I traveled through the land,
I find your people full of strange reports,
Possessed with rumors, full of idle dreams,
Not knowing what they fear, but full of fear.
And here's a prophet that I brought with me   115
From the village of Pomfret, whom I found
With many hundreds treading on his heels,
To whom he sung in rude, harsh-sounding rhymes
That before next Ascension Day at noon
Your highness should relinquish up your crown.   120

KING JOHN

You idle dreamer, why did you say so?

PETER

I can foresee the truth shall fall out so.

KING JOHN

Hubert, away with him, and lock him up!

And on Ascension Day at noon, just when

He says I'll yield my crown, string him up high.   125

Right now take him to jail and then come back,

For I still need your help.

Exit Hubert with Peter

Gentle cousin,

Have you already heard who has arrived?

BASTARD

The French, my lord. Men's mouths are full of it.   130

And I ran into Pembroke and Salisbury,

And they're outraged, their eyes are burning coals.

They have a posse going to find the grave

Of Arthur, whom they say was killed tonight

On your suggestion.   135

KING JOHN

Gentle cousin, go

And thrust yourself into their company.

I need to find a way to win them back.

Bring them to me.

BASTARD

I will go seek them out.   140

KING JOHN

And let me have no home-grown enemies

While foreign terrorists invade my towns.

Be Mercury, put feathers on your boots,

And fly like thought from them to me again.

BASTARD

The spirit of the time will teach me speed.   145

He leaves

KING JOHN

Spoke like a true quick-witted gentleman!
Go after him, because he may just need
Some back-up, some muscle, a body-guard.
That's your new job.

MESSENGER

With all my heart, my liege!   150

Messenger exits

KING JOHN

My mother dead!

Enter Hubert

HUBERT

My lord, they say five moons were seen tonight,
Four stayed in place, the fifth one spun around
The other four in wonderful motion!

KING JOHN

Fake news!   155

HUBERT

Old men and old crones in the streets
Are speculating on it dangerously.
They're saying Arthur's dead, they're gossiping
And when they talk of him, they shake their heads,
And whisper rumors in each other's ears.   160
I saw a blacksmith standing, listening,
As his iron on his anvil lost its heat.
With open mouth, he swallowed the tailor's news.
The tailor, with his scissors and his tape,
Stood in his slippers, which he had thrown on   165
Because he couldn't pause to lace his boots.

71

He warned of the battalions of the French
Gathering in warlike order down in Kent,
And as they spoke another citizen
Cut short that tale and talked of Arthur's death.   170
KING JOHN
    Why do you want to burden me with fears?
    Why do you speak so much of Arthur's death?
    You murdered him. It's true I had my reasons
    To wish him dead, but you had none to kill him.
HUBERT
    Why order me to do what you don't want?   175
KING JOHN
    It is the curse of kings to be surrounded
    By sycophants who call a whim a warrant,
    And on the pretense of authority
    To understand a law, to know the meaning
    Of awesome royalty and its mere frowns —   180
    To misinterpret our "moods" as "orders."
HUBERT (Shows him the warrant)
    Here is your hand and seal for what I did.
KING JOHN
    Oh, when the final tale of heaven and earth
    Is written, then this letter, signed and sealed,
    Condemns us to eternal damnation.   185
    The sight of someone evil is often
    So suggestive. Had you not been nearby,
    Staring at me with your contorted face,
    This murder wouldn't have come into my mind.
    But taking note of your disfigurement,   190
    Sensing your willingness to kill the child,
    I hinted slightly at young Arthur's death,
    And you, being a total brown-noser,

Took it upon yourself to kill a prince!

HUBERT

What the hell?   195

KING JOHN

If only you had shook your head, or paused

When I spoke darkly what I'd merely mused,

If you had turned a doubtful eye to me,

Told me to speak exactly what I meant,

Deep shame would have silenced me, made me stop   200

And your doubts would have spawned such doubts in me.

Instead you dared presume to read my mind,

Supplanting my thoughts with thoughts of your own.

Consequently, your harsh hand committed

The action which neither of us could speak.   205

Get out of my sight, and never look at me.

My nobles have left, and my realm faces ruin,

And in my own body, this human flesh,

This kingdom, this prison of blood and breath,

Hostility and civil tumult reigns   210

Between my conscience and that child's death.

HUBERT

I'll make a peace between your soul and you.

Young Arthur is alive. This hand of mine

Is still a virgin, keeps its innocence,

Isn't tainted with crimson drops of blood.   215

Within my heart there has never entered

The dreadful motion of a murderous thought,

And you have slandered my humanity.

I would never butcher an innocent child.

KING JOHN

Arthur's alive? High-tail it to the peers!   220

Throw this water upon their fiery rage,

And make them tame and pledge obedience!
And also, please forgive what I have said
About the way you look. I was pissed off,
And I saw you through very angry eyes.   225
No need to answer. But bring back to me
The angry lords with all expedient haste.
I conjure you but slowly, now, run fast!

All exit

ACT 4 ◆ SCENE 3
BEFORE THE CASTLE

Enter Arthur, on the walls, disguised as a ship-boy

ARTHUR

The wall is high, but I'll attempt escape.
Good ground, be merciful, and don't hurt me.
There's no one here who knows me. If there were,
This sailor's suit has quite disguisèd me.
I am afraid, and yet I'll venture it.   5
If I survive, and do not break my neck,
I'll find a thousand tricks to get away.
As good to die and go, as die and stay.

(leaps down)

Oh *merde*! My uncle's spirit is in these stones!
Heaven, take my soul, and England keep my bones.   10

Dies

Enter Pembroke, Salisbury, and Bigot with a letter

SALISBURY

I'll meet the Dauphin at St. Edmundsbury.
It's in our interest and we must embrace
His generous offer at this perilous time.

PEMBROKE

Who brought this letter from the Cardinal?

74

SALISBURY

    The Count Melun, a noble lord of France,   15

    Whose secret "intel" about the Dauphin

    Is more persuasive than the cardinal's words.

BIGOT

    Tomorrow morning, let us meet Melun.

Enter the Bastard

BASTARD

    Once more today well-met, unhappy lords.

    The king requests your presence with him now.   20

SALISBURY

    The king has disappointed all of us.

    We will not reinforce John's tattered cloak

    With fabric of our strength, nor serve the man

    That leaves a bloody footprint where he walks.

    Return, and tell him so. We know the worst.   25

BASTARD

    Whatever you think you know, kind words are best.

SALISBURY

    Our griefs and not our manners reason now.

BASTARD

    But there is little reason for your grief.

    Therefore, there's reason to show manners now.

PEMBROKE

    Sir, our righteous anger takes precedence.   30

BASTARD

    If true, to hurt yourself, but no one else.

SALISBURY

    This is his prison.

(sees Arthur)

    What's that lying there?

PEMBROKE

Oh, Death made proud with pure and princely beauty!

The earth has not a hole to hide this crime.   35

SALISBURY

Murder, as hating what himself has done,

Here lays it open to urge on revenge.

BIGOT

Or, when he doomed this beauty to a grave,

Found it too precious-princely for a grave.

SALISBURY *(to the Bastard)*

Richard, what do you think? Have you seen this?   40

Or have you read or heard, or could you think

That you do see? This is the very top,

The height, the crest, or crest unto the crest,

Of murder's arms. This is the bloodiest shame,

The wildest savagery, the vilest stroke,   45

That ever wide-eyed wrath or staring rage

Presented to the tears of soft remorse.

PEMBROKE

This makes all murders past seem justified.

And this, so singular and terrible,

Shall give a holiness, a purity,   50

To the most unimaginable crimes.

BASTARD

It is a damnèd and a bloody work,

The graceless action of a heavy hand,

If that it be the work of any hand.

SALISBURY

If that it be the work of any hand?   55

It is the shameful work of Hubert's hand,

The practice and the purpose of the king,

From whose obedience I free my soul,

Kneeling before this ruin of sweet life
And breathing to its breathless excellence   60
The incense of a vow, a holy vow,
No more to taste the pleasures of this world,
Till I have made a glory of this hand
By giving it the worship of revenge.

PEMBROKE AND BIGOT *(together)*

Our souls religiously confirm your words.   65

Enter Hubert

HUBERT

Lords, I am hot with haste in seeking you.
Prince Arthur lives. The king now sends for you.

SALISBURY

Oh, he is bold and blushes not at Death!
Beat it, you hateful villain. Out of here!

HUBERT

I am no villain.   70

SALISBURY *(draws his sword)*

Must I be the law?

BASTARD

Your sword is bright, sir. Put it up again.

SALISBURY

Not till I sheathe it in that murderer's skin.

HUBERT

Stand back, Lord Salisbury. Stand back, I say.
By heaven, I think my sword's as sharp as yours.   75
I would not have you, lord, forget yourself,
Or tempt the danger of my true defense,
In case, responding to your rage, I forget
Your worth, your greatness, and nobility.

BIGOT

You piece of shit! Threaten a nobleman?   80

SALISBURY

You are a murderer!

HUBERT

Don't make me one.

I am none yet. Whose tongue says so speaks false.

PEMBROKE

Cut him to pieces.

BASTARD *(drawing)*

Keep the peace, I say.   85

SALISBURY

Move, or I will kill you, Faulconbridge.

BASTARD

If you but frown at me, or twitch your foot,

I'll strike you dead. Put up your sword instead.

BIGOT

What will you do, renowned Faulconbridge?

Defend a villain and a murderer?   90

HUBERT

Lord Bigot, I am none!

BIGOT

Who killed this prince?

HUBERT

It's not an hour since I left him alive.

I honored him, I loved him and will weep

My length of life out for his sweet life's loss.   95

He weeps

SALISBURY

Don't trust those cunning tear-drops in his eyes,

For villainy can always cry on cue.

He's so well-trained he leads us to believe

His river of tears will prove his innocence.

Away with me, all you whose souls despise   100

The unclean odor of a slaughter-house,

For I am sickened with this smell of sin.

BIGOT

Let's meet the Dauphin at St. Edmundsbury.

SALISBURY

Let King John know that we've now joined the French.

The English Lords leave

BASTARD

Here's a good world! Knew you of Arthur's death?   105

Beyond the infinite and boundless reach

Of mercy, if indeed you murdered him,

You are damned, Hubert.

HUBERT

Do but hear me, Sir.

BASTARD

Ha! I'll tell you what.   110

You are completely damned. No-one's more damned

Than you shall be, if you murdered this child.

HUBERT

I swear on my soul —

BASTARD

If you even consented

To this most cruel act, you should despair.   115

And if you need a rope, the smallest thread

That spider ever twisted from her womb

Will serve to strangle you, a twig will be a beam

To hang yourself. Or if you'd rather drown,

Put one small drop of water in a spoon   120

And it shall be as all the ocean,

Enough to stifle such a villain up.

HUBERT

If I in act, consent, or sin of thought,

Am guilty of stealing that sweet boy's breath,
Let hell invent new pains to torture me. 125
He was alive.

BASTARD

Then take him in your arms.
I am astonished, and I lose my way
Among the thorns and dangers of this world.

(Hubert lifts Arthur's body)

How easy can one take all England up! 130
From forth this morsel of dead royalty,
The life, the right, the truth of all this realm
Has fled to heaven, and England now remains
To tug and scramble and part by the teeth
The varied interests of proud-swelling state. 135
Now for the bare-picked bone of majesty,
The dogs of war bristle and lick their chops,
And snarl into the gentle eyes of peace.
How happy is he, whose cloak is waterproof
And can withstand this deluge. Take him away, 140
And follow me with speed. I'll find King John.
A thousand businesses are brief in hand,
And heaven itself does frown upon this land.

They exit,
Hubert carrying Arthur's little body

ACT 5 ◆ SCENE 1

KING JOHN'S PALACE

Enter King John and Pandulph with the crown, and their Attendants

KING JOHN

    Thus have I yielded up into your hand

    The circle of my glory.

PANDULPH *(handing the crown to John)*

    Take again.

    My hand represents the pope and bestows

    Your sovereign greatness and authority.   5

KING JOHN

    Now keep your holy word. Go meet the French,

    And on the pope's behalf use all your power

    To stop their marches before we're destroyed.

    Our discontented counties do rebel,

    Our people quarrel with my right to rule,   10

    Swearing allegiance and their loyalty

    To stranger blood, to foreign royalty.

    It's up to you to calm and to subdue

    This inundation of unrest and bile.

PANDULPH

    It was my breath that blew this tempest up   15

    After your stubborn treatment of the pope,

    But since you have converted back to Rome,

    My tongue shall hush again this storm of war

    And make fair weather in your war-torn land.

    On this Ascension Day, remember well,   20

    Upon your oath of service to the pope,

    Now I will make the French lay down their arms.

All exit except John

KING JOHN

This is Ascension Day? Didn't the prophet
Promise that by Ascension Day at noon
I should give up my crown? Even so I have. 25
I did suppose it should be on constraint
But heaven be thanked, it is by my free will.

Enter the Bastard

BASTARD

All Kent's surrendered. No one there holds out
But Dover Castle. London has received
Like a kind host, the Dauphin and his powers. 30
Your nobles will not listen, and are gone
To offer service to your enemy,
And wild amazement hurries up and down
The dwindling number of your anxious friends.

KING JOHN

Would my lords not return to me again 35
After they learned young Arthur was alive?

BASTARD

They found him dead and thrown into the streets.

KING JOHN

That villain Hubert told me that he lived!

BASTARD

So, on my soul, for all he knew, he did.
But why are you suddenly so depressed? 40
Be great in act, as you have been in thought.
Don't let the world see fear and sad distrust
Govern the motion of your kingly eye.
What, will they seek the lion in his den
And scare him there, and make him tremble there? 45
Hell, no. Let's find our enemy and plan

To meet displeasure farther from our doors.

We'll rumble him before he gets closer.

KING JOHN

The pope's ambassador was just with me

And he and I made such a happy deal, 50

So much so that he promised to destroy

The Dauphin's powers.

BASTARD

Oh, what a shameful deal.

Should we, upon the footing of our land,

Send memorandums and make compromise, 55

Instead of beating back that beardless boy?

That pampered, pompadoured French philistine?

Shall he find no resistance? Lord, let's fight!

KING JOHN

You have my blessing. I put you in charge.

BASTARD

Away then, with good courage! 60

(aside) Yet I know

Our troops may soon confront a prouder foe.

They exit

ACT 5 ◆ SCENE 2

THE DAUPHIN'S CAMP AT ST. EDMUNDSBURY

Enter (in arms) Lewis the Dauphin, Salisbury, Melun,
Pembroke, Bigo, ,and Soldiers

DAUPHIN *(handing a paper to Melun)*

My lord Melun, let this be copied out

And keep it safe for our remembrance.

Return the first draft to these English lords,

Let them know that we wrote everything down,

So they and we, by having both these drafts, 5

May know just why we took this sacrament.

SALISBURY

Upon our side it never shall be broken.
And, noble Dauphin, even though we swear
A voluntary zeal and strong belief
In your proceedings, yet believe me, prince,   10
I am not pleased that such a cursèd time
Should seek to heal the canker of one wound
By making many. Oh, it grieves my soul
That I must draw this weapon from my side
To be a widow-maker! Oh, and here —   15
It is a pity, oh, my grieving friends,
That we, the sons and daughters of this land
Were born to see so sad an hour as this.

He weeps

DAUPHIN

A noble temper you do show in this.
Let me wipe off these honorable tears   20
That fall like silver raindrops on your cheeks.
Lift up your brow, renownèd Salisbury.
Come, come, for you will plunge your hand as deep
Into the purse of rich prosperity
As I myself do. So will everyone   25
Who knits his sinews to the strength of mine.

(trumpet sounds)

And even now, I think I hear an angel.

Enter Pandulph

Here comes the cardinal, Rome's ambassador,
To bring to us divine news from the pope
And on our action set the name of right   30
With holy breath.

84

PANDULPH

    Hail, noble prince of France.

    The news is this, King John hath reconciled

    Himself with Rome, his spirit hath come in

    That once opposed the Roman Catholic Church.   35

    Therefore, fold up thy threatening flags and banners,

    And tame the savage spirit of wild war,

    That, like a lion fostered up at hand,

    It may lie gently at the foot of peace.

DAUPHIN

    Your grace will pardon me, I won't back down.   40

    I am too high-born to be bossed around,

    To be a secondary at control

    To any sovereign state throughout the world.

    Your breath first kindled the dead coal of wars

    Between this chastised kingdom and myself,   45

    And now it's grown too large to be blown out

    With that same weak breath that ignited it.

    You taught me how to know the face of right,

    You thrust this enterprise into my heart,

    And now you come to tell me John has made   50

    His peace with Rome? What is that peace to me?

    Am I Rome's slave? What money has Rome spent?

    What men provided? Or what weapons sent

    To supplement this war? Is't not myself

    Who's bearing all the cost? Who else but I,   55

    And those on my side, have a genuine stake

    In this business and can maintain this war?

    Don't I hold here the best cards in this game

    Of poker that we play for sovereignty?

    Do I now fold and forfeit up my hand?   60

    No, on my soul, it never shall be said.

PANDULPH

You only see the outside of this plan.

DAUPHIN

Outside or inside, I will not retreat.

(a trumpet sounds)

What lusty trumpet now calls out to us?

Enter the Bastard

BASTARD

According to our diplomatic law   65

Let me have audience. I am sent to speak,

My holy Lord of Milan, from the king.

I come to learn how you have bargained here,

And, from your answer, I'll then know

If I respond to you as friend or foe.   70

PANDULPH

The Dauphin is willful and obstinate.

He says point-blank he'll not lay down his arms.

BASTARD

By all the blood that ever fury breathed,

The youth says well! Now, hear our English King,

He is prepared and with good reason too.   75

This beardless sauciness of boyish troops,

The king just smiles at, and is resolved

To cudgel France and make it take the lash,

And you degenerates, you ingrate rebels

Of your dear mother England, blush for shame!   80

For your own ladies and innocent girls

Like amazons come dancing to our drums —

DAUPHIN

Stop your blather and turn your face in peace.

Our time is too precious to be squandered

On such a windbag —   85

PANDULPH

Give me leave to speak.

BASTARD

I am not done —

DAUPHIN

We will listen to neither!

Strike up the drums, and let the tongue of war

Plead for our interest, and our presence here.   90

BASTARD

Indeed, your drums being beaten will cry out,

And so will you, being beaten. Do but start

An echo with the clamor of your drum,

And we will answer with a steady beat

That will reverberate and drown you out.   95

Sound but another, and another shall,

Loudly as yours, rattle the firmament

And mock the deep-mouthed thunder. For at hand,

Not trusting to this lamely limping priest,

Is warlike John, and on his forehead sits   100

A bare-ribbed Death, whose purpose is this day

To feast upon whole thousands of the French.

DAUPHIN

Strike up our drums to find this danger out.

BASTARD

And you will find it, Dauphin, have no doubt.

Exit all

ACT 5 ◆ SCENE 3
THE FIELD OF BATTLE
Trumpets are heard
Enter King John and Hubert

KING JOHN

How goes the day with us? Oh tell me, Hubert?

HUBERT

Badly, I fear. How fares your majesty?

KING JOHN

This fever that I've had for several days

Still burns me up. And my heart is in pain.

Enter a Messenger

MESSENGER

My lord, your bastard kinsman, Faulconbridge,   5

Desires your majesty to leave the field

And send him word by me which way you go.

KING JOHN

Tell Faulconbridge we'll meet at Swinstead Abbey.

MESSENGER

You can relax, for all of the supplies

That were expected by the Dauphin here,   10

Were wrecked three nights ago on Goodwin Sands.

The French have lost all hope, and are fatigued.

KING JOHN

Oh, me. This tyrant fever burns me up,

And will not let me welcome such good news.

Set on toward Swinstead. To my stretcher straight.   15

Weakness overtakes me, and I feel faint.

Exit all

ACT 5 ◆ SCENE 4
ANOTHER PART OF THE FIELD
Enter Salisbury, Pembroke, and Bigot

SALISBURY

I did not think the King had such strong friends.

PEMBROKE

Up once again. Put spirit in the French.

If they miscarry, we miscarry too.

SALISBURY

That misbegotten devil, Faulconbridge,

In spite of spite, alone upholds the day.   5

PEMBROKE

They say King John's near death and leaves the field.

Enter Melun, wounded, led by a soldier

MELUN *(to the soldier)*

Lead me to the rebellious English lords.

SALISBURY

When we were happy, we had other names.

PEMBROKE

It is the Count Melun.

SALISBURY

He's close to death.   10

MELUN

Fly, noble English, for you are betrayed!

Seek out King John and kneel before his feet,

For, if the French be lords of this loud day,

Lewis will recompense the pains you take

By cutting off your heads. Thus he has sworn,   15

And he had many witnesses, like me.

SALISBURY

May this be possible? May this be true?

MELUN

Have I not hideous death within my view?
Retaining but a smidgen's worth of life,
What in the world should make me now deceive,   20
Since I must lose the use of all deceit?
I say again, if Lewis wins the day,
He has sworn those eyes of yours will not behold
Another morning dawning in the East.
Because my *grand-père* was an Englishman,   25
Awakes my conscience to confess all this.
In gratitude, I pray you carry me
Far from the noise and tumult of the field.

SALISBURY

My arm shall give you help to bring you there,
For I do see the cruel pangs of death   30
Clear in your eye. Away, my friends! New flight,
And happy newness, that puts old wrongs right.

They exit, leading off Melun

ACT 5 ◆ SCENE 5
THE FRENCH CAMP

Enter Lewis, the Dauphin, and one soldier

DAUPHIN

I thought the sun was never going to set,
It stayed and made the whole horizon blush,
As England stumbled back on their own ground
In faint retire. Oh, bravely we marched off,
And with a volley of triumphant shot,   5
After such bloody toil, we said good night,
And wound our tattered banners into balls,
Last in the field, and almost lords of it.

Enter a Messenger

MESSENGER

Where is my prince, the Dauphin?

DAUPHIN

Here. What news?   10

MESSENGER

The Count Melun is dead. The English lords

By him persuaded change their loyalties,

And your supply, for which you have such need,

Is cast away and sunk on Goodwin Sands.

DAUPHIN

Terrible news! Anathema to my heart!   15

I did not think to be so sad tonight

As this has made me. Who was it that said

King John escaped an hour or two before

The stumbling night did part our weary powers?

MESSENGER

Whoever spoke it, it is true, my lord.   20

DAUPHIN

Well, keep a lookout and take care tonight.

The day shall not be up so soon as I

To try the fair adventure of tomorrow.

They exit

ACT 5 ◆ SCENE 6

AN OPEN PLACE IN THE NEIGHBORHOOD
OF SWINSTEAD ABBEY

Enter the Bastard and Hubert in the dark

HUBERT

Who's there? Speak up! Speak quickly, or I'll shoot.

BASTARD

A friend. And what are you?

HUBERT

An Englishman.

BASTARD

Where are you headed?

HUBERT

Why d'you give a damn?   5

BASTARD

Hubert, I think?

HUBERT

And you think perfectly.

But who are you?

BASTARD

I dare you take a guess.

But you'll befriend me so much as to think   10

That I'm descended from Plantagenets.

HUBERT

That's my mistake! Brave soldier, pardon me,

For I walk here in the black brow of night,

To find you out.

BASTARD

Brief, then, and what's the news?   15

HUBERT

The king, I fear, is poisoned by a monk.

BASTARD

How did this happen? Who tasted his food?

HUBERT

The self-same monk, a scheming little shit,

Whose bowels then exploded. That's our proof.

King John is conscious and may yet recover.   20

BASTARD

Who did you leave to take care of the king?

HUBERT

Haven't you heard? The lords are all come back,
And brought Prince Henry in their company,
At whose request the king has pardoned them,
And they surround his royal majesty.   25

BASTARD

Hubert, we lost half of our troops tonight.
These Lincoln Washes have been our undoing.
Crossing these flats, the rising tide came in,
Myself and my stallion barely escaped.
Let's go, you first. Conduct me to the king,   30
I hope he won't be dead before I come.

They exit

ACT 5 ◆ SCENE 7
THE ORCHARD AT SWINSTEAD ABBEY
Enter Prince Henry, Salisbury, and Bigot

PRINCE HENRY

It is too late. The life of all his blood
Is thoroughly poisoned, and his pure brain,
Which some suppose is where the soul resides,
Does by the garbled comments that he makes
Predict the ending of his earthly life.   5

Enter Pembroke

PEMBROKE

His highness is still conscious and believes
That if he's brought into the open air
It would perhaps allay the burning pain
Of the poison which makes his fever climb.

PRINCE HENRY

Let him be brought into the orchard here.   10
Is he still ranting?

93

PEMBROKE

He is more cogent
Than when you left him. He's even singing.

PRINCE HENRY

It's strange that death should sing.
I am the cygnet to this pale faint swan,   15
Who chants a doleful hymn to his own death,
And from the organ-pipe of frailty sings
His soul and body to their lasting rest.

SALISBURY

Be of good comfort, prince, for you are born
To set a form upon the chaos here.   20

Enter Attendants, carrying King John in a chair

KING JOHN

Good lord, at last my soul has elbow room,
It would not out at windows nor at doors.
There is so hot a summer in my bosom,
That all my bowels crumble up to dust.
I am a scribbled form drawn with a pen   25
Upon a parchment, and against this fire
I shrivel and shrink up.

PRINCE HENRY

How do you feel?

KING JOHN

I'm poisoned, ill-used, dead, forsook, cast off,
And none of you will bid the winter come   30
To thrust his icy fingers in my mouth,
Nor let my kingdom's rivers take their course
Through my burned bosom, nor entreat the North
To make his bleak winds kiss my parchèd lips
And comfort me with cold. I don't ask much,   35
I beg cold comfort, and you're so aloof

And so ungrateful, you deny me that.

PRINCE HENRY

    Oh that there were some virtue in my tears

    That might relieve you.

KING JOHN

    The salt in them is hot.   40

    Within me is a hell, and there the poison

    Is, as a fiend, confined to tyrannize

    My un-reprievable, condemnèd blood.

Enter the Bastard

BASTARD

    I'm hot and sweaty as a racing horse,

    With spleen of speed to see your majesty!   45

KING JOHN

    Oh cousin, you have come to close my eyes,

    The tackle of my heart is cracked and burnt,

    And all the shrouds wherewith my life should sail

    Are turnèd to one thread, one little hair.

    My heart has one poor string to stay it by,   50

    Which holds but till your news be uttered,

    And then all this you see is but a clod

    And module of confounded royalty.

BASTARD

    The Dauphin is already on his way,

    God only knows how we shall answer him.   55

    Last night the best of my battalions,

    After we'd won and came home from the field —

King John dies

SALISBURY

    You breathe your dead news in as dead an ear.

    My liege, my lord! But now a king, now thus.

PRINCE HENRY

Even so must I run on, and even so stop. 60

What guarantee is there, what hope, what stay,

When this was once a king, and now is clay?

BASTARD

Are you gone, so? I do but stay behind

To do the office for you of revenge

And then my soul shall wait on you in heaven, 65

As it on earth has been your servant still.

(to the Lords)

Now, now, you stars that move in your right spheres,

Where are your powers? Show now your mended faiths,

And instantly return with me again.

Straight let us seek, or straight we shall be sought. 70

The Dauphin rages at our very heels.

SALISBURY

It seems you know not, then, so much as we.

The Cardinal Pandulph is within at rest,

Who half an hour since came from the Dauphin,

And brings us peaceful offers from the French. 75

BASTARD

Let it be so. And you, my noble prince,

With other princes that may best be spared,

Shall wait upon your father's funeral.

PRINCE HENRY

At Worcester must his body be interred,

For he so willed it. 80

BASTARD

He shall go there then.

And happily may your sweet self put on

The lineal state and glory of the land,

To whom with all submission, on my knee

I do bequeath my faithful services   85
And true subjection, everlastingly.

He kneels

SALISBURY

And the like offer of our love we make,
To rest without blemish for evermore.

They kneel to the prince

PRINCE HENRY

I have a kind soul that would give you thanks   90
And knows not how to do it but with tears.

They rise

BASTARD

Let's pay the time all necessary woe,
Though we've already seasoned it with grief.
This England never did, nor never shall,
Lie at the proud foot of a conqueror,   95
Except when it first helped to wound itself.
Now that our princes have returned to us,
Come the three corners of the world in arms,
And we will shock them. Naught shall make us rue,
If England to itself do rest but true.   100

They exit, carrying the body of King John

END